HISTC
IS A SET OF
LIES AGREED UPON

WRITINGS ABOUT THE
GREAT
NAPOLEON BONAPARTE

By

VARIOUS

CONTENTS

THE DEATH OF NAPOLEON

By Isaac Mclellan

Wild was the night, yet a wilder night
Hung round the soldier's pillow;
In his bosom there waged a fiercer fight
Than the fight on the wrathful billow.

A few fond mourners were kneeling by,
The few that his stern heart cherished;
They knew, by his glazed and unearthly eye,
That life had nearly perished.

They knew by his awful and kingly look,
By the order hastily spoken,
That he dreamed of days when the nations shook,
And the nations' hosts were broken.

He dreamed that the Frenchman's sword still slew,
And triumphed the Frenchman's eagle,
And the struggling Austrian fled anew,
Like the hare before the beagle.

The bearded Russian he scourged again,
The Prussian's camp was routed,
And again on the hills of haughty Spain
His mighty armies shouted.

Over Egypt's sands, over Alpine snows,
At the pyramids, at the mountain,
Where the wave of the lordly Danube flows,
And by the Italian fountain,

On the snowy cliffs where mountain streams
Dash by the Switzer's dwelling,
He led again, in his dying dreams,
His hosts, the proud earth quelling.

Again Marengo's field was won,
And Jena's bloody battle;
Again the world was overrun,
Made pale at his cannon's rattle.

He died at the close of that darksome day,
A day that shall live in story;
In the rocky land they placed his clay,
And left him alone with his glory."

A POEM FROM
Poems That Every Child Should Know, 1904

NAPOLEON I
(BONAPARTE)

By Pierre-Louis-Théophile-Georges Goyau

Emperor of the French, second son of Charles Marie Bonaparte and Maria Lætitia Ramolino, b. at Ajaccio, in Corsica, 15 August, 1769; d. on the Island of St. Helena, 5 May, 1821. His childhood was spent in Corsica; at the end of the year 1778 he entered the college of Autun, in 1779 the military school of Brienne, and in 1783 the military school of Paris. In 1785, when he was in garrison at Valence, as a lieutenant, he occupied his leisure with researches into the history of Corsica and read many of the philosophers of his time, particularly Rousseau. These studies left him attached to a sort of Deism, an admirer of the personality of Christ, a stranger to all religious practices, and breathing defiance against "sacerdotalism" and "theocracy". His attitude under the Revolution was that of a citizen devoted to the new ideas, in testimony of which attitude we have his scolding letter, written in 1790, to Battafuoco, a deputy from the Corsican *noblesse*, whom the "patriots" regarded as a traitor, and also a work published by Bonaparte in 1793, "Le Souper de Beaucaire", in which he takes the side of the Mountain in the Convention against the Federalist tendencies of the Girondins.

His military genius revealed itself in December, 1793, when he was twenty-four years of age, in his recapture of Toulon from the English. He was made a general of brigade in the artillery, 20 December, and in 1794 contributed to Masséna's victories in Italy. The political suspicions aroused by his friendship with the younger Robespierre after 9 Thermidor of the Year III (27

July, 1794), the intrigues which led to his being removed from the Italian frontier and sent to command a brigade against the Vendeans in the west, and ill health, which he used as a pretext to refuse this post and remain in Paris, almost brought his career to an end. He contemplated leaving France to take command of the sultan's artillery. But in 1795 when the Convention was threatened, Bonaparte was selected for the duty of pouring grapeshot upon its enemies from the platform of the church of Saint Roch (13 Vendémiaire, Year IV). He displayed great moderation in his hour of victory, and managed to earn at once the gratitude of the Convention and the esteem of its enemies.

The Campaign in Italy

On 8 March, 1798, he contracted a civil marriage with the widow of Alexandre de Beauharnais, Marie Joséphine Rose Tascher de la Pagerie, who was born in Martinique, in 1763, of a family originally belonging to the neighbourhood of Blois. In the same month Napoleon set out for Italy, where the Directory, prompted by Carnot, had appointed him commander in chief against the First Coalition. The victory of Montenotte, over the Austrians commanded by Beaulieu, and those of Millesimo, Dego, Ceva, and Mondovi, over Colle's Piedmontese troops, forced Victor Amadeus, King of Sardinia, to conclude the armistice of Cherasco (28 April, 1796). Wishing to effect a junction on the Danube with the Army of the Rhine, Bonaparte spent the following May in driving Beaulieu across Northern Italy, and succeeded in pushing him back into the Tyrol. On 7 May he was ordered by the Directory to leave half of his troops in Lombardy, under Kellermann's command, and march with the other half against Leghorn, Rome, and Naples. Unwilling to share the glory with Kellermann, Bonaparte replied by tendering his resignation, and the order was not insisted on. In a proclamation to his soldiers (20 May, 1796) he declared his intention of leading them to the banks of the Tiber to chastise those who had "whetted the daggers of civil war in France" and "basely assassinated" Basseville, the French minister, to "re-establish the Capitol, place there in honour the statues of heroes who had made themselves famous", and to "arouse the Roman people benumbed by many centuries of bondage". In June he entered the Romagna, appeared at Bologna and Ferrara, and made prisoners of several prelates. The Court of Rome demanded an armistice, and Bonaparte, who was far from eager for this war against the Holy See, granted it. The Peace of Bologna (23 June, 1796) obliged the Holy See to give up Bologna and Ferrara to French occupation, to pay twenty one million francs, to surrender 100 pictures, 500 manuscripts, and the busts of Junius and Marcus Brutus. The Directory thought these terms too easy, and when a prelate was sent to Paris to negotiate the treaty, he was told that as an indispensable condition of peace, Pius VI must revoke the Briefs relating to the Civil Constitution of the clergy and to the Inquisition. The Pope refused, and negotiations were broken off; they failed again at Florence, where an attempt had been made to renew them.

During these *pourparlers* between Paris and Rome, Bonaparte repulsed the repeated efforts of the Austrian Wurmser to reconquer Lombardy. Between 1 and 5 August, Wurmser was twice beaten at Lonato and again at Castiglione; between 8 and 15 September, the battles of Roveredo, Primolano, Bassano, and San Giorgio forced Wurmser to take refuge in Mantua, and on 16 October Bonaparte created the Cispadan Republic at the expense of the Duchy of Modena and of the Legations, which were pontifical territory. Then, 24 October, he invited Cacault, the French minister at Rome, to reopen negotiations with Pius VI "so as to catch the old fox"; but on 28 October he wrote to the same Cacault: "You may assure the pope that I have always been opposed to the treaty which the Directory has offered him, and above all to the manner of negotiating it. I am more ambitious to be called the preserver than the destroyer of the

Holy See. If they will be sensible at Rome, we will profit by it to give peace to that beautiful part of the world and to calm the conscientious fears of many people." Meanwhile the arrival in Venetia of the Austrian troops under Alvinzi caused Cardinal Busca, the pope's secretary of state, to hasten the conclusion of an alliance between the Holy See and the Court of Vienna; of this Bonaparte learned through intercepted letters. His victories at Arcoli (17 November, 1796) and Rivoli (14 January, 1797) and the capitulation of Mantua (2 February, 1797), placed the whole of Northern Italy in his hands, and in the spring of 1797 the Pontifical States were at his mercy.

The Directory sent him ferocious instructions. "The Roman religion", they wrote, "will always be the irreconcilable enemy of the Republic; first by its essence, and next, because its servants and ministers will never forgive the blows which the Republic has aimed at the fortune and standing of some, and the prejudices and habits of others. The Directory requests you to do all that you deem possible, without rekindling the torch of fanaticism, to destroy the papal Government, either by putting Rome under some other power or" which would be still better "by establishing some form of self government which would render the yoke of the priests odious." But at the very moment when Bonaparte received these instructions he knew, by his private correspondence, that a Catholic awakening was beginning in France. Clarke wrote to him: "We have become once more Roman Catholic in France", and explained to him that the help of the pope might perhaps be needed before long to bring the priests in France to accept the state of things resulting from the Revolution. Considerations such as these must have made an impression on a statesman like Bonaparte, who, moreover, at about this period, said to the parish priests of Milan: "A society without religion is like a ship without a compass; there is no good morality without religion." And in February, 1797, when he entered the Pontifical States with his troops, he forbade any insult to religion, and showed kindness to the priests and the monks, even to the French ecclesiastics who had taken refuge in papal territory, and whom he might have caused to be shot as émigrés. He contented himself with levying a great many contributions, and laying hands on the treasury of the Santa Casa at Loretto. The first advances of Pius VI to his "dear son General Bonaparte" were met by Bonaparte's declaring that he was ready to treat. "I am treating with this rabble of priests [*cette prêtraille*], and for this once Saint Peter will again save the Capitol", he wrote to Joubert, 17 February, 1797. The Peace of Tolentino was negotiated on 19 February; the Holy See surrendered the Legations of Bologna, Ferrara, and Ravenna, and recognized the annexation of Avignon and the Comtat Venaissin by France. But Bonaparte had taken care not to infringe upon the spiritual power, and had not demanded of Pius VI the withdrawal of those Briefs which were offensive to the Directory. As soon as the treaty was signed he wrote to Pius VI to express to him "his perfect esteem and veneration"; on the other hand, feeling that the Directory would be displeased, he wrote to it: "My opinion is that Rome, once deprived of Bologna, Ferrara, the Romagna, and the thirty millions we are taking from her, can no longer exist. The old machine will go to pieces of itself." And he proposed that the Directory should take the necessary steps with the pope in regard to the religious situation in France.

Then, with breathless rapidity, turning back towards the Alps, and assisted by Joubert, Masséna, and Bernadotte, he inflicted on Archduke Charles a series of defeats which forced Austria to sign the preliminaries of Leoben (18 April, 1797). In May he transformed Genoa into the Ligurian Republic; in October he imposed on the archduke the Treaty of Campo Formio, by which France obtained Belgium, the Rhine country with Mainz, and the Ionian Islands, while Venice was made subject to Austria. The Directory found fault with this last stipulation; but Bonaparte had already reached the point where he could act with independence and care little for what the politicians at

Paris might think. It was the same with his religious policy: he now began to think of invoking the pope's assistance to restore peace in France. A note which he addressed to the Court of Rome, 3 August, 1797, was conceived in these terms: "The pope will perhaps think it worthy of his wisdom, of the most holy of religions, to execute a Bull or ordinance commanding priests to preach obedience to the Government, and to do all in their power to strengthen the established constitution. After the first step, it would be useful to know what others could be taken to reconcile the constitutional priests with the non constitutional."

While Bonaparte was expressing himself thus, the Councils of the Five Hundred and the Ancients were passing a law to recall, amnesty, and restore to their civil and political rights the priests who had refused to take the oath of the Civil Constitution of the Clergy. But Directors Barrès, Rewbell, and Lareveillère Lépeaux, considering that this act jeopardized the Republic, employed General Augereau, Bonaparte's lieutenant, to carry out the *coup d'état* of 18 Fructidor against the Councils (4 Sept., 1797), and France was once more a prey to a Jacobin and anti-Catholic policy. These events were immediately echoed at Rome, where Joseph Bonaparte, the general's brother, and ambassador from the Directory, was asked by the latter, to favour the Revolutionary party. Disturbances arose: General Duphot was killed in Joseph Bonaparte's house (28 December, 1797), and the Directory demanded satisfaction from the Holy See. General Bonaparte had just returned to Paris, where he apparently confined himself to his functions as a member of the Institute (Scientific Section). He was by no means anxious to lead the expedition against Rome, which the Directory was projecting, and contented himself with giving Berthier, who commanded it, certain instructions from a distance.

The Campaign in Egypt

While in Paris, Bonaparte induced the Directory to take up the plan of an expedition to Egypt. His object was to make the Mediterranean a French lake, by the conquest of Malta and the Nile Valley, and to menace England in the direction of India. He embarked on 19 May, 1798. The taking of Malta (10 June), of Alexandria (2 July), the battle of the Pyramids (21 July), gave Bonaparte the uncontested mastery of Cairo. At Cairo he affected a great respect for Islam; reproached with this later on, he replied: "It was necessary for General Bonaparte to know the principles of Islamism, the government, the opinions of the four sects, and their relations with Constantinople and Mecca. It was necessary, indeed, for him to be thoroughly acquainted with both religions, for it helped him to win the affection of the clergy in Italy and of the ulemas in Egypt."

The French troops in Egypt were in great danger when the naval disaster of Aboukir, inflicted by Nelson, had cut them off from Europe. Turkey took sides with England: in the spring of 1799, Bonaparte made a campaign in Syria to strike both Turkey and England. Failing to effect the surrender of Acre, and as his army was suffering from the plague (May, 1799), he had to make his way back to Egypt. There he re-established French prestige by the victory of Aboukir (25 July, 1799), then, learning that the Second Coalition was gaining immense successes against the armies of the Directory, he left Kléber in Egypt and returned secretly to France. He landed at Fréjus, 9 October, 1799, and was in Paris seven days later. Besides certain political results, the expedition to Egypt had borne fruit for science: Egyptology dates its existence from the creation of the Institute of Egypt (*Institut d'Egypte*) by Bonaparte.

Bonaparte, First Consul

While Bonaparte was in Egypt, the religious policy of the Directory had provoked serious troubles in France. Deportations of priests were multiplying; Belgium, where 6000 priests were proscribed, was disturbed; the Vendée, Normandy, and the departments of the South were rising. France was angry and uneasy. Spurred on by his brother Lucien, president of the Five Hundred, allied with Directors Sieyès and Roger Ducos, Bonaparte caused Directors Gohier and Moulins to be imprisoned, and broke up the Five Hundred (18 Brumaire; 9-10 November, 1799). The Directorial Constitution was suppressed, and France thenceforward was ruled by three consuls. First Consul Bonaparte put into operation the Constitution known as that of the Year VIII, substituted for the departmental administrators elected by the citizens, others appointed by the Executive Power, and reorganized the judicial and financial administrations. He commissioned the Abbé Bernier to quiet the religious disturbance of the Vendeans, and authorized the return of the non juring priests to France on condition of their simply promising fidelity to the laws of the republic. Then, to make an end of the Second Coalition, he entrusted the Army of Germany to Moreau, and, himself taking command of the Army of Italy, crossed the Great St. Bernard (13-16 May, 1800) and, with the co operation of Desaix, who was mortally wounded, crushed the Austrians (14 June, 1800) between Marengo and San Giuliano at the very spot he had marked on the map in his study in the Tuileries. The Peace of Lunéville, concluded with Austria, 9 February, 1801, extended the territory of France to 102 departments.

Bonaparte spent the years 1801 and 1802 effecting internal reforms in France. A commission, established in 1800, elaborated a new code which, as the "Code Napoléon", was to be promulgated in 1804, to formally introduce some of the "principles of 1789" into French law, and thus to complete the civil results of the Revolution. But it was Napoleon's desire that, in the new society which was the issue of the Revolution, the Church should have a place, and consciences should be set at rest. The Concordat with the Holy See was signed on 17 July, 1801; it was published, together with the Organic Articles, as a law, 16 April, 1802. The former of these two acts established the existence of the Church in France, while the other involved the possibility of serious interference by the State in the life of the Church. Napoleon never said, "The Concordat was the great fault of my reign." On the contrary, years afterwards, at St. Helena, he considered it his greatest achievement, and congratulated himself upon having, by the signature of the Concordat, "raised the fallen altars, put a stop to disorders, obliged the faithful to pray for the Republic, dissipated the scruples of those who had acquired the national domains, and broken the last thread by which the old dynasty maintained communication with the country." Fox, in a conversation with Napoleon at this period, expressed astonishment at his not having insisted upon the marriage of priests: "I had, and still have, to accomplish peace", Napoleon replied, "theological controversies are allayed with water, not with oil." The Concordat had wrecked the hopes of those who, like Mme de Staël, had wished to make Protestantism the state religion of France; and yet the Calvinist Jaucourt, defending the Organic Articles before the Tribunat, gloried in the definitive recognition of the Calvinist religion by the state. The Jewish religion was not recognized until later (17 March, 1808), after the assembly of a certain number of Jewish delegates appointed by the prefects (29 July, 1806) and the meeting of the Great Sanhedrim (10 February - 9 April, 1807); the State, however, did not make itself responsible for the salaries of the rabbis. Thus did the new master of France regulate the religious situation in that country.

On 9 April, 1802, Caprara was received for the first time by Bonaparte in the official capacity of Pius VII's , and before the first consul took an oath which, according to the text subsequently published by the "Moniteur", bound him to observe the constitution, the laws, statutes, and customs of the republic, and nowise to derogate from the rights, liberties, and privileges of the Gallican Church. This was a painful surprise for the Vatican, and Caprara declared that the words about Gallican liberties had been interpolated in the "Moniteur".

Another painful impression was produced at the Vatican by the attitude of eight constitutional priests whom Bonaparte had nominated to bishoprics, and to whom Caprara had granted canonical institution, and who afterwards boasted that they had never formally abjured their adhesion to the Civil Constitution of the clergy. In retaliation, the Roman curia demanded of the constitutional parish priests a formal retractation of the Civil Constitution, but Bonaparte opposed this and when Caprara insisted, declared that if Rome pushed matters too far the consuls would yield to the desire of France to become Protestant. Talleyrand spoke to Caprara in the same sense, and the legate desisted from his demands. On the other hand, though Bonaparte had at first been extremely irritated by the allocution of 24 May, 1802, in which Pius VII demanded the revision of the Organic Articles, he ended by allowing it to be published in the "Moniteur" as a diplomatic document. A spirit of conciliation on both sides tended to promote more cordial relations between the two powers. The proclamation of Bonaparte as consul for life (August, 1802) increased in him the sense of his responsibility towards the religion of the country, and in Pius VII the desire to be on good terms with a personage who was advancing with such long strides towards omnipotence.

Bonaparte took care to gain the attachment of the revived Church by his favours. While he dissolved the associations of the Fathers of the Faith, the Adorers of Jesus, and the Panarists, which looked to him like attempts to restore the Society of Jesus, he permitted the reconstitution of the Sisters of Charity, the Sisters of St. Thomas, the Sisters of St. Charles, and the Vatelotte Sisters, devoted to teaching and hospital work, and made his mother, Madame Lætitia Bonaparte, protectress of all the congregations of hospital sisters. He favoured the revival of the Institute of the Christian Schools for the religious instruction of boys; side by side with the *lycées*, he permitted secondary schools under the supervision of the prefects, but directed by ecclesiastics. He did not rest content with a mere strict fulfilment of the pecuniary obligations to the Church to which the Concordat had bound the State; in 1803 and 1804 it became the custom to pay stipends to canons and *desservants* of succursal parishes. Orders were issued to leave the Church in possession of the ecclesiastical buildings not included in the new circumscription of parishes. Though the State had not bound itself to endow diocesan seminaries, Bonaparte granted the bishops national estates for the use of such seminaries and the right to receive donations and legacies for their benefit; he even founded, in 1804, at the expense of the State, ten metropolitan seminaries, re-established, with a government endowment, the Lazarist house for the education of missionaries, and placed the Holy Sepulchre and the Oriental Christians under the protection of France.

As to the temporal power of the popes Bonaparte at this period affected a somewhat complaisant attitude towards the Holy See. He restored Pesaro and Ancona to the pope, and brought about the restitution of Benevento and Pontecorvo by the Court of Naples. After April, 1803, Cacault was replaced, as his representative at Rome, by one of the five French ecclesiastics to whom Pius VII had consented to grant the purple late in 1802. This ambassador was no other than Bonaparte's own uncle, Cardinal Joseph Fesch, whose secretary for a short time was Chateaubriand, recently made famous by his "La génie du Christianisme". One of Bonaparte's grievances against Cacault was a saying attributed to the latter: "How many sources of his glory would cease if Bonaparte ever chose to play Henry VIII!" Even in those days of harmony Cacault had a presentiment that the Napoleonic policy would yet threaten the dignity of the

Holy See. The idea of a struggle with England became more and more an imperious obsession of Bonaparte's mind. The Peace of Amiens (25 March, 1802) was only a truce: it was broken on 22 May, 1803, by Mortier's invasion of Hanover and the landing of the English in French Guiana. Napoleon forthwith prepared for his gigantic effort to lay the ban of Europe on England. The Duc d'Enghien, who was suspected of complicity with England and the French Royalists, was carried off from Ettenheim, a village within the territory of Baden, and shot at Vincennes, 21 March, 1804, and one of Cardinal Fesch's first acts as ambassador at Rome was to demand the extradition of the French *émigré* Vernègues, who was in the service of Russia, and whom Bonaparte regarded as a conspirator.

NAPOLEON EMPEROR

The Coronation

While the Third Coalition was forming between England and Russia, Bonaparte caused himself to be proclaimed hereditary emperor (30 April 18 May, 1804), and at once surrounded himself with a brilliant Court. He created two princes imperial (his brothers Joseph and Louis), seven permanent high dignitaries, twenty great officers, four of them ordinary marshals, and ten marshals in active service, a number of posts at Court open to members of the old nobility. Even before his formal proclamation as emperor, he had given Caprara a hint of his desire to be crowned by the pope, not at Reims, like the ancient kings, but at Notre Dame de Paris. On 10 May, 1804, Caprara warned Pius VII of this wish, and represented that it would be necessary to answer yes, in order to retain Napoleon's friendship. But the execution of the Duc d'Enghien had produced a deplorable impression in Europe; Royalist influences were at work against Bonaparte at the Vatican, and the pope was warned against crowning an emperor who, by the Constitution of 1804, would promise to maintain "the laws of the Concordat", in other words, the Organic Articles. Pius VII and Consalvi tried to gain time by dilatory replies, but these very replies were interpreted by Fesch at Rome, and by Caprara at Paris, in a sense favourable to the emperor's wishes. At the end of June, Napoleon I joyfully announced, at the Tuileries, that the pope had promised to come to Paris. Then Pius VII tried to obtain certain religious and political advantages in exchange for the journey he was asked to make. Napoleon declared that he would have no conditions dictated to him; at the same time he promised to give new proofs of his respect and love for religion, and to listen to what the pope might have to submit. At last the cleverness of

Talleyrand, Napoleon's minister of foreign affairs, conquered the scruples of Pius VII; he declared, at the end of September, that he would accept Napoleon's invitation if it were officially addressed to him; he asked only that the ceremony of consecration should not be distinct from the coronation proper, and that Napoleon would undertake not to detain him in France. Napoleon had the invitation conveyed to Pius VII, not by two bishops, as the pope expected, but by a general; and before setting out for France, Pius VII signed a conditional act of abdication, which the cardinals were to publish in case Napoleon should prevent his returning to Rome; then he began his journey to France, 2 November, 1804.

Napoleon would not accord any solemn reception to Pius VII; surrounded by a hunting party, he met the pope in the open country, made him get into the imperial carriage, seating himself on the right, and in this fashion took him to Fontainebleau. Pius VII was brought to Paris by night. The whole affair nearly fell through at the last moment. Pius VII informed Josephine herself, on the eve of the day set for the coronation of the empress, that she had not been married to Napoleon in accordance with the rules of religion. To the great annoyance of the emperor, who was already contemplating a divorce, in case no heir were born to him, and was displaying a lively irritation against Josephine, Pius VII insisted upon the religious benediction of the marriage; otherwise, there was to be no coronation. The religious marriage ceremony was secretly performed at the Tuileries, on the first of December, without witnesses, not during the night, but at about four o'clock in the afternoon, by Fesch, grand almoner of the imperial household. As Welschinger has proved, Fesch had previously asked the pope for the necessary dispensations and faculties, and the marriage was canonically beyond reproach. On 2 December the coronation took place. Napoleon arrived at Notre Dame later than the hour appointed. Instead of allowing the pope to crown him, he himself placed the crown on his own head and crowned the empress, but, out of respect for the pope, this detail was not recorded in the "Moniteur". Pius VII, to whom Napoleon granted but few opportunities for conversation, had a long memoranda drawn up by Antonelli and Caprara, setting forth his wishes; he demanded that Catholicism should be recognized in France as the dominant religion; that the divorce law should be repealed; that the religious communities should be re-established; that the Legations should be restored to the Holy See. Most of these demands were to no purpose: the most important of the very moderate concessions made by the emperor was his promise to substitute the Gregorian Calendar for that of the Revolution after 1 January, 1806. When Pius VII left Paris, 4 April, 1805, he was displeased with the emperor.

But the Church of France acclaimed the emperor. He was lauded to the skies by the bishops. The parish priests, not only in obedience to instructions, but also out of patriotism, preached against England, and exhorted their hearers to submit to the conscription. The splendour of the Napoleonic victories seemed, by the enthusiasm with which it inspired all Frenchmen, to blind the Catholics of France to Napoleon's false view of the manner in which their Church should be governed. He had reorganized it; he had accorded it more liberal pecuniary advantages than the Concordat had bound him to; but he intended to dominate it. For example, in 1806 he insisted that all periodical publications of a religious character should be consolidated into one, the "Journal des curés", published under police surveillance. On 15 August, 1806, he instituted the Feast of St. Napoleon, to commemorate the martyr Neopolis, or Neopolas, who suffered in Egypt under Diocletian. In 1806 he decided that ecclesiastical positions of importance, such as cures of souls of the first class, could be given only to candidates who held degrees conferred by the university, adding that these degrees might be refused to those who were notorious for their "ultramontane ideas or ideas dangerous to authority". He demanded the publication of a single catechism for the whole empire, in which catechism he was called "the image of God upon earth," "the Lord's anointed",

21

and the use of which was made compulsory by a decree dated 4 April, 1806. The prisons of Vincennes, Fenestrelles, and the Island of Sainte Marguerite received priests whom the emperor judged guilty of disobedience to his orders.

The Great Victories; Occupation of Rome; Imprisonment of Pius VII (1805-09)

After 1805 relations between Pius VII and Napoleon became strained. At Milan, 26 May, 1805, when Napoleon, as King of Italy, took the Iron Crown of Lombardy, he was offended because the pope did not take part in the ceremony. When he asked Pius VII to annul the marriage which his brother Jerome Bonaparte had contracted, at the age of nineteen with Elizabeth Patterson of Baltimore, the pope replied that the decrees of the Council of Trent against clandestine marriages applied only where they had been recognized, and the reply constituted one more cause of displeasure for the emperor, who afterwards, in 1806, obtained an annulment from the complaisant ecclesiastical authorities of Paris. And when Consalvi, in 1805, complained that the French Civil Code, and with it the divorce law, had been introduced into Italy, Napoleon formally refused to make any concession.

The great war which the emperor was just then commencing was destined to be an occasion of conflict with the Holy See. Abandoning the preparations which he had made for an invasion of England (the Camp of Boulogne), he turned against Austria, brought about the capitulation of Ulm (20 October, 1805), made himself master of Vienna (13 November), defeated at Austerlitz (2 December, 1805) Emperor Francis I and Tsar Alexander. The Treaty of Presburg (26 December, 1805) united Dalmatia to the French Empire and the territory of Venice to the Kingdom of Italy, made Bavaria and Wurtemberg vassal kingdoms of Napoleon, enlarged the margravate of Baden, and transformed it into a grand duchy, and reduced Austria to the valley of the Danube. The victory of Trafalgar (21 October, 1805) had given England the mastery of the seas, but from that time forward Napoleon was held to be the absolute master of the Continent. He then turned to the pope, and demanded a reckoning of him.

To prevent a landing Russian and English troops in Italy, Napoleon, in October, 1805, had ordered Gouvion Saint Cyr to occupy the papal city of Ancona. The pope, lest the powers hostile to Napoleon might some day reproach him with having consented to the employment of a city of the Pontifical States as a base of operations, had protested against this arbitrary exercise of power: he had complained, in a letter to the emperor (13 November, 1805), of this "cruel affront", declared that since his return from Paris he had "experienced nothing but bitterness and sorrow", and threatened to dismiss the French ambassador.

But the treaty of Presburg and the dethronement of the Bourbons of Naples by Joseph Bonaparte and Masséna (January, 1806), changed the European and the Italian situation. From Munich Napoleon wrote two letters (7 January, 1806), one to Pius VII, and the other to Fesch, touching his intentions in regard to the Holy See. He complained of the pope's ill will, tried to justify the occupation of Ancona, and declared himself the true protector of the Holy See. "I will be the friend of Your Holiness", he concluded, "whenever you consult only your own heart and the true friends of religion." His letter to Fesch was much more violent: he complained of the refusal to annul Jerome's marriage, demanded that there should no longer be any minister either of Sardinia or of Russia in Rome, threatened to send a Protestant as his ambassador to the pope, to appoint a senator to command in Rome and to reduce the pope to the status of mere Bishop of Rome, claimed that the pope should treat him like Charlemagne, and assailed "the pontifical camarilla which prostituted religion". A reply from Pius VII (29 January, 1806), asking for the return of Ancona and the Legations let loose Napoleon's fury. In a letter to Pius VII (13 February), he declared: "Your Holiness is the sovereign of Rome but I am its emperor; all my enemies ought to be yours"; he insisted that the pope should drive English, Russian, Sardinian, and Swedish subjects out of his dominions, and close his ports to the ships of those powers with which France was at war; and he complained of the slowness of the Curia in granting canonical institution to bishops in France and Italy. In a letter to Fesch he declared that, unless the pope acquiesced he would reduce the condition of the Holy See to what it had been before Charlemagne.

An official note from Fesch to Consalvi (2 March, 1806) defined Napoleon's demands; the cardinals were in favour of rejecting them, and Pius VII, in a very beautiful letter, dated 21 March, 1806, remonstrated with Napoleon, declared that the pope had no right to embroil himself with the other states, and must hold aloof from the war; also, that there was no emperor of Rome. "If our words", he concluded, "fail to touch Your Majesty's heart we will suffer with a resignation conformable to the Gospel, we will accept every kind of calamity as coming from God." Napoleon, more and more irritated, reproached Pius VII for having consulted the cardinals before answering him, declared that all his relations with the Holy See should thenceforward be conducted through Talleyrand, ordered the latter to reiterate the demands which the pope had just rejected, and replaced Fesch as ambassador at Rome with Alquier, a former member of the Convention. Then the emperor proceeded from words to deeds. On 6 May, 1806, he caused Città Vecchia to be occupied. Learning that the pope, before recognizing Joseph Bonaparte as King of Naples, wished Joseph to submit to the ancient suzerainty of the Holy See over the Neapolitan Kingdom, he talked of "the spirit of light headedness" (*esprit de vertige*) which prevailed at Rome, remarked that, when the pope thus treated a Bonaparte as a vassal, he must be tired of wielding the temporal power, and directed Talleyrand to tell Pius VII that the time was past when the pope disposed of crowns. Talleyrand was informed (16 May, 1806) that, if Pius VII would not

24

recognize Joseph, Napoleon would no longer recognize Pius VII as a temporal prince. "If this continues", Napoleon went on to say, "I will have Consalvi taken away from Rome." He suspected Consalvi of having sold himself to the English. Early in June, 1806, he seized Benevento and Pontecorvo, two principalities which belonged to the Holy See, but which were shut in by the Kingdom of Naples.

Yielding before the emperor's wrath, Consalvi resigned his office: Pius VII unwillingly accepted his resignation, and replaced him with Cardinal Casoni. But the first dispatch written by Casoni under Pius VII's dictation confirmed the pope's resistance to the emperor's behests. Napoleon then violently apostrophized Caprara, in the presence of the whole court, threatening to dismember the Pontifical States, if Pius VII did not at once, "without ambiguity or reservation", declare himself his ally (1 July, 1806). A like ultimatum was delivered, on 8 July, to Cardinal Casoni by Alquier. But Continental affairs were claiming Napoleon's attention, and the only immediate result of his ultimatum was the emperor's order to his generals occupying Ancona and Città Vecchia, to seize the pontifical revenues in those two cities. On the other hand, the constitution of the Imperial University (May, 1806), preparing for a state monopoly of teaching, loomed up as a peril to the Church's right of teaching, and gave the Holy See another cause for uneasiness.

The Confederation of the Rhine, formed by Napoleon out of fourteen German States (12 July, 1806), and his assertion of a protectorate over the same, resulted in Francis II's abdication of the title of emperor of Germany; it its place Francis took the title of emperor of Austria. Thus ended, under the blows dealt it by Napoleon, that Holy Roman Germanic Empire which had exerted so great an influence over Christianity in the Middle Ages. The pope and the German emperor had long been considered as sharing between them the government of the world in the name of God. Napoleon had definitively annihilated one of these "two halves of God", as Victor Hugo has termed them. Frederick William II of Prussia became alarmed, and in October, 1806, formed, with England and Russia, the Fourth Coalition. The stunning victories of Auerstädt, won by Davoust, and Jena, won by Napoleon (14 October, 1806), were followed by the entry of the French into Berlin, the king of Prussia's flight to Königsberg, and the erection of the Electorate of Saxony into a kingdom in alliance with Napoleon. From Berlin itself Napoleon launched a decree (21 November, 1806) by which he organized the Continental blockade against England, aiming to close the whole Continent against English commerce. Then, in 1807, penetrating into Russia, he induced the tsar by means of the battles of Eylau (8 February, 1807) and Friedland (14 June, 1807), to sign the Peace of Tilsit (8 July, 1807). The empire was at its apogee; Prussia had been bereft of its Polish provinces, given to the King of Saxony under the name of the Grand Duchy of Warsaw; the Kingdom of Westphalia was being formed for Jerome Bonaparte, completing the series of kingdoms given since 1806 to the emperor's brothers - Naples having been assigned to Joseph, and Holland to Louis. A series of principalities and duchies, "great fiefs", created all over Europe for his marshals, augmented the might and prestige of the empire. At home, the emperor's personal power was becoming more and more firmly established; the supervision of the press more rigorous; summary incarcerations more frequent. He created an hereditary nobility as an ornament to the throne.

To him it was something of a humiliation, that the Court of Rome persisted in holding aloof, politically, from the great conflicts of the nations. He began to summon the pope anew. He had already, soon after Jena, called Mgr Arezzo to him from Saxony, and in menacing fashion had bidden him go and demand of Pius VII that he should become the ally of the empire; once more Pius VII had replied to Arezzo that the pope could not consider the enemies of France his enemies. Napoleon also accused the pope of hindering the ecclesiastical reorganization of Germany, and of not making provision for the dioceses of Venetia. His grievances were multiplying. On 22 July, 1807, he wrote to Prince Eugène, who governed Milan as his viceroy, a letter intended to be shown to the pope: "There were kings before there were popes", it ran. "Any pope who denounced me to Christendom would cease to be pope in my eyes; I would look upon him as Antichrist. I would cut my peoples off from all communication with Rome. Does the pope take me for Louis the Pious? What the Court of Rome seeks is the disorder of the Church, not the good of religion. I will not fear to gather the Gallican, Italian, German and Polish Churches in a council to transact my business [*pour faire mes affaires*] without any pope, and protect my peoples against the priests of Rome. This is the last time that I will enter into any discussion with the Roman priest rabble [*la prêtraille romaine*]". On 9 August Napoleon wrote again to Prince Eugène, that, if the pope did anything imprudent, it would afford excellent grounds for taking the Roman States away from him. Pius VII, driven to bay, sent Cardinal Litta to Paris to treat with Napoleon: the pope was willing to join the Continental blockade, and suspend all intercourse with the English, but not to declare war against them. The pope even wrote to Napoleon (11 September, 1807) inviting him to come to Rome. The emperor, however, was only seeking occasion for a rupture, while the pope was seeking the last possible means of pacification.

Napoleon refused to treat with Cardinal Litta, and demanded that Pius VII should be represented by a Frenchman, Cardinal de Bayanne. Then he pretended that Bayanne's powers from the pope were not sufficient. And while the pope was negotiating with him in good faith, Napoleon, without warning, caused the four pontifical Provinces of Macerata, Spoleto, Urbino, and Foligno to be occupied by General Lemarrois (October, 1807). Pius VII then revoked Cardinal Bayanne's powers. It as evident that, not only did Napoleon require of him an offensive alliance against England, but that the Emperor's pretensions, and those of his new minister of foreign affairs, Champagny, Talleyrand's successor, were now beginning to encroach upon the domain of religion. Napoleon claimed that one third of the cardinals should belong to the French Empire; and Champagny let it be understood that the emperor would soon demand that the Holy See should respect the "Gallican Liberties", and should abstain from "any act containing positive clauses or reservations calculated to alarm consciences and spread divisions in His Majesty's dominions". Henceforth it was the spiritual authority that Napoleon aspired to control. Pius VII ordered Bayanne to reject the imperial demands. Napoleon then (January, 1808) decided that Prince Eugène and King Joseph should place troops at the disposition of General Miollis, who was ordered to march on Rome. Miollis at first pretended to be covering the rear of the Neapolitan army, then he suddenly threw 10,000 troops into Rome (2 February). Napoleon wrote to Champagny that it was necessary "to accustom the people of Rome and the French troops to live side by side, so that, should the Court of Rome continue to act in an insensate way, it might insensibly cease to exist as a temporal power, without anyone noticing the change". Thus it may be said that, in the beginning of 1808, Napoleon's plan was to keep Rome.

In a manifesto to the Christian powers, Pius VII protested against this invasion; at the same time, he consented to receive General Miollis and treated him with great courtesy. Champagny, on 3 February, again insisted on the pope's becoming the political ally of Napoleon, and Pius VII refused. The instructions given to Miollis became more severe every day: he seized printing presses, journals, post offices; he decimated the Sacred College by having seven cardinals conducted to the frontier, because Napoleon accused them of dealing with the Bourbons of the two Sicilies, then, one month later, he expelled fourteen other cardinals from Rome because they were not native subjects of the pope. Cardinal Doria Pamphili, who had been appointed secretary of state, in February, 1808, was also expelled by Miollis; Pius VII now had with him only twenty one cardinals, and the papal Government was disorganized. He broke off all diplomatic relations with Napoleon, recalled Bayanne and Caprara from Paris, and uttered his protest in a consistorial allocution delivered in March. Napoleon, on his side, recalled Alquier from Rome. The struggle between pope and emperor was taking on a tragic character.

On 2 April Napoleon signed two decrees: one annexed to the Kingdom of Italy "in perpetuity" the Provinces of Urbino, Ancona, Macerata, and Camerino; the other ordered all functionaries of the Court of Rome who were natives of the Kingdom of Italy to return to that kingdom, under pain of confiscation of their property. Pius VII protested before all Europe against this decree, on 19 May, and, in an instruction addressed to the bishops of the provinces which Napoleon was lopping off from his possessions, he denounced the religious "indifferentism" of the imperial Government, and forbade the faithful of those provinces to take the oath of allegiance to Napoleon or accept any offices from him. Miollis retaliated, 12 June, by driving Gavrielli, the new secretary of state, out of Rome. Pius VII then replaced Gavrielli with Cardinal Pacca, reputed an opponent of France; on 11 July he delivered a very spirited allocution, which, in spite of the imperial police, was circulated throughout Europe; and Pacca, on 24 August, directed a note against the institution of the "Civic Guard" - an idea recently conceived by Miollis - in which Miollis was compelling even the pope's soldiers to enroll. On 6 September, 1808, Miollis sent two officers to the Quirinal to arrest Pacca; Pius VII interposed, declaring that they should not arrest Pacca without arresting the pope, and that in future the secretary of state should sleep at the Quirinal, which was closed to all the French.

The definitive execution of Napoleon's projects against the Holy See was retarded by the wars which occupied him during the year 1808. When he transferred his brother Joseph from the Throne of Naples to that of Spain, Spain rose, and the English invaded Portugal. Dupont's capitulation, at Baylen (20 July,

1808), and Junot's at Cintra (30 August, 1808), were painful reverses for French arms. Napoleon, having made an alliance with the tsar in the celebrated interview of Erfurt (27 September - 14 October, 1808), hastened to Spain. There he found a people whose spirit of resistance was exasperated all the more because they believed themselves to be fighting for their liberty and the integrity of their faith as much as for their country. In November he gained the victories of Burgos, Espinosa, Tudela, and Somo Sierra, and reopened the gates of Madrid for Joseph; on 21 February Saragossa was taken by the French armies after an heroic resistance. A Fifth Coalition was formed against Napoleon: he returned from Spain and, rushing across Bavaria, bombarded and took Vienna (11 13 May, 1809). On the day after the victory he devoted some of his leisure hours to thinking about the pope.

For some time Murat, who in 1808 had replaced Joseph as King of Naples, had been ready to support Miollis whenever Napoleon should judge that the hour had come to incorporate Rome with the empire. On 17 May, 1809, Napoleon issued from Schönbrunn two decrees in which, reproaching the popes for the ill use they had made of the donation of Charlemagne, his "august predecessor", he declared the Pontifical States annexed to the empire, and organized, under Miollis, a council extraordinary to administer them. On 10 June Miollis had the Pontifical flag, which still floated over the castle of St. Angelo, lowered. Pius VII replied by having Rome placarded with a Bull excommunicating Napoleon. When the emperor received news of this (20 June) he wrote to Murat: "So the pope has aimed an excommunication against me. No more half measures; he is a raving lunatic who must be confined. Have Cardinal Pacca and other adherents of the pope arrested." In the night of 5 6 July, 1809, Radet, a general of gendarmerie, by the orders of Miollis, entered the Quirinal, arrested Pius VII and Pacca, gave them two hours to make their preparations, and took them away from Rome at four in the morning. Pius VII was taken to Savona, Pacca to Fenestrella.

Meanwhile Napoleon, completing the work of crushing Austria, had been the victor at Essling (21 May, 1809) and at Wagram (6 July, 1809), and the Peace of Vienna (15 October, 1809) put the finishing touch to the mutilation of Austria by handing over Carniola, Croatia, and Friuli to France, at the same time obliging the Emperor Francis to recognize Joseph as King of Spain. The young german, Staps, who attempted to assassinate Napoleon at Schöenbrunn (13 October), died crying: "Long live Germany!"

Discussion with the captive Pius VII; Second Marriage; Ecclesiastical Councils of 1809 and 1811

The conflict with his prisoner, the pope, was another embarrassment, a new source of anxiety to the emperor. At first he took all possible steps to prevent the public from hearing of what had happened at Rome: the "Moniteur" made not the slightest allusion to it; the newspapers received orders to be silent. He also wished his excommunication to be ignored; the newspapers must be silent on this point also; but the Bull of Excommunication, secretly brought to Lyons, was circulated in France by members of the Congregation, a pious association, founded 2 February, 1801, by Père Delpuits, a former Jesuit. Alexis de Noailles and five other members of the Congregation were arrested by the emperor's command, and his anger extended to all the religious orders. He wrote (12 September, 1809) to Bigot de Préameneu, minister of public worship: "If on 1 October there are any missions or congregations still in France, I will hold you responsible." The celebrated Abbé Frayssinous had to discontinue his sermons; the Lazarists dispersed; the Sulpicians were threatened. Napoleon consulted Bigot de Préameneu as to the expediency of laying the Bull before the Council of State, but abstained from doing so.

It was not long, however, before he had to face an enormous

difficulty: there were more than twenty bishoprics vacant, and Pius VII declared to Fesch, to Caprara, and to Maury that, so long as he was a prisoner, so long as he could not communicate freely with his natural counsellors, the cardinals, he would not provide for the institution of the bishops. Thus the life of the Church of France was partially suspended. In November, 1809, Napoleon appointed an "ecclesiastical council" to seek a solution of the difficulty. With Fesch as president, this council included as members Cardinal Maury, Barral, Archbishop of Tours, Duvoisin, Bishop of Nantes, Emery, Superior of S. Sulpice, Bishops Canaveri of Vercelli, Bourlier of Evreux, Mannay of Trèves, and the Barnabite Fontana. Bigot de Préameneu, in the name of the emperor, laid before the council several sets of questions relating to the affairs of Christendom in general, then to those of France, and lastly to those of Germany and Italy, and to the Bull of Excommunication.

In the preamble to its replies, the council gave voice to a petition for the absolute liberty of the pope and the recall of the cardinals. It declared that if a general council were assembled for the settlement of the religious questions then pending, the pope's presence at the council would be necessary, and that a national council would not have sufficient authority in questions affecting the whole Catholic Church. It also declared that the pope could not complain of any essential violation of the Concordat, that, when he advanced his temporal spoliation, as one reason for his refusal to institute the bishops canonically, he was confounding the temporal order with the spiritual, that the temporal sovereignty was only an accessory of the papal authority, that the invasion of Rome was not a violation of the Concordat, and that the national council would interpose an appeal from the Bull of Excommunication either to the general council or to the pope better informed. The manner in which canonical institution might be secured for the bishops, if the pope should continue his resistance, was twice discussed. Urged by the Government, the council admitted that, taking the circumstances into consideration, the conciliary institution given by a metropolitan to his suffragans, or by the senior suffragan to a new metropolitan, might possibly be recognized by a national council as, provisionally, a substitute for pontifical Bulls. Emery, thinking the council too lenient, refused to endorse the answers, which were sent to Napoleon on 11 January, 1810.

On 17 February, 1810, the Act regulating the Roman territory and future condition of the pope, introduced by Régnault de Saint Jean d'Angély, was passed unanimously by the senate. The Papal States, in accordance with this decree, were to form two departments; from Rome, which was declared the first city of the empire, the prince imperial was to take his title of king. The emperor, already crowned once at Notre Dame, was to go within ten years to be crowned at St. Peter's. The pope was to have a revenue of two millions. The empire was to charge itself with the maintenance of the Sacred Congregation of Propaganda. The pope, on his accession, must promise to do nothing contrary to the four articles of the Gallican Church. Another Act of the Senate, of 25 February, 1810, made the Declaration of 1682 a general law of the empire. Thus did Napoleon flatter himself that he would reduce the papacy to servitude and bring Pius VII to live in Paris. He even prepared a letter to Pius VII in which he told him: "I hold in execration the principles of the Bonifaces and the Gregorys. It is my mission to govern the West; do not meddle with it." This letter he would have had taken to the pope by bishops who were to give notice to Pius VII that in future the popes must swear allegiance to Napoleon, as of yore to Charlemagne, and to inform him that he himself would be dispensed from this obligation, but that he must undertake not to reside at Rome. Napoleon expected in this way to bend the pope to his will. Wiser counsellors, however, prevailed upon him not to send this insulting letter. Nevertheless, to carry out his plan of removing the papal throne from Rome, he ordered Miollis to compel all the cardinals who were still at Rome to set out for Paris, and to have the Vatican archives transported thither. In 1810 there were twenty seven Roman cardinals in Paris; he lavished gifts upon them, invited them to the court festivals, and wished them to write and urge Pius VII to yield; but, following the advice of Consalvi, the cardinals refused.

It was in the midst of these bitter conflicts with the church that, Napoleon desiring an heir, resolved to divorce Josephine. Ever since the end of 1807 Metternich had been aware of the reports that were current about the emperor's approaching divorce. On 12 December, 1807, Lucien Bonaparte had vainly endeavored to obtain from Josephine her consent to this divorce; some time after, Fouché had made a similar attempt with no better success. In December, 1809, at Fontainebleau, in the presence of Prince Eugène, Josephine's son, the emperor induced her to consent; on 15 December, this was solemnly proclaimed in the throne room, in the presence of the Court, in an address delivered by Napoleon, and another read by the unhappy Josephine, who was prevented by her tears from finishing it. The Act of the Senate (16 December), based on a report of Lacépède, the naturalist, himself a member of the Senate, ratified the divorce. Napoleon then thought of marrying the tsar's sister. But Metternich, getting wind of this project, made Laborde and Schwarzenberg sound the Tuileries to see if Napoleon would marry an Austrian archduchess. The idea pleased Napoleon. The Court of Vienna, however, first required that the spiritual bond between Napoleon and Josephine should be severed.

This bond the pope alone was competent to dissolve; Louis XII had had recourse to Alexander VI; Henry IV to Clement VIII; but Napoleon, excommunicated by his prisoner Pius VII, could not apply to him. Cambacérès, the arch chancellor, sent for the diocesan officials of Paris and explained to them that the marriage of Napoleon and Josephine had been invalid in consequence of the absence of the parish priest of the two parties and of witnesses. In vain did they object that only the pope could decide such a case; they were told to commence proceedings, and be quick about it. On 26 December, the promoter of the case, Rudemare, begged Cambacérès to submit the matter to the ecclesiastical council over which Fesch presided. On 2 January, 1810, Cambacérès sent a request to the official, Boislesve, for a declaration of nullity of the marriage, alleging, this time, that there had been absence of consent on Napoleon's part. On the next day the ecclesiastical council replied that if the defect of Napoleon's consent could be proved to the officiality, the marriage would be null and void. Cambacérès wished to produce Fesch, Talleyrand, Duroc, and Berthier as witnesses. The testimony of Fesch was very confused; he explained that the pope had given him the necessary dispensations to bless the marriage; that two days later he had given Josephine a marriage certificate; that the emperor had then upbraided him, declaring to him that he (the emperor) had only agreed to this marriage in order to quiet the empress, and that it was, moreover, impossible for him to renounce his hopes of direct descendants. The other two witnesses told how Napoleon had repeatedly expressed the conviction that he was not bound by this marriage and that he regarded the ceremony only as "a mere concession to circumstances [*acte de pure circonstance*] which ought not to have any effect in the future".

On 9 January the diocesan authorities declared the marriage null and void, on the ground of the absence of the lawful parish priest and of witnesses; it pronounced this decision only in view of the "difficulty in the way of having recourse to the visible head of the Church, to whom it has always belonged in fact to pronounce upon these extraordinary cases." The promoter Rudemare had concluded with the recommendation that the tribunal should at least lay a precept upon the two parties to repair the defect of form which had vitiated their marriage; Boilesve, the official, refrained from proffering this invitation. Rudemare then appealed to the metropolitan authorities on this point. On 12 January, 1810, the official, Lejeas, with much greater complaisance, admitted both the grounds of nullity advanced by Cambacérès - that is, not only the defect of form, but also the

35

defect of the emperor's consent. He alleged that the civil marriage of Napoleon and Josephine had been annulled by the decree of the Senate, that by the concordatory laws (*lois concordataires*) the religious marriage ought to follow the civil, and that the Church could not now ask two parties who were no longer civilly married to repair the defects of form in their religious marriage. Thus, he declared, the marriage was religiously annulled. It may be noted here that the Catholic Church cannot be held responsible for the excessive complaisance shown in this matter by the ecclesiastical council and the diocesan authorities of Paris. On 21 January, 1810, Napoleon resolved to ask for the hand of Marie Louise. The French ambassador at Vienna, at the request of the Archbishop of Vienna, gave him his word of honour that the sentence pronounced by the diocesan authorities of Paris was legal. At last all the religious obstacles to the celebration of the new marriage were disposed of.

It took place on 1 April, 1810, but thirteen of the cardinals then in Paris refused to be present. These thirteen cardinals were turned away when they presented themselves at the Tuileries two days later; the minister of public worship informed them that they were no longer cardinals, that they no longer had any right to wear the purple; the minister of police forwarded them, two by two, to small country towns; their pensions were suppressed, their property sequestrated. People called them "the black cardinals". The bishops and priests of the Roman States were treated with similar violence; nineteen out of thirty two bishops refused the oath of allegiance to the emperor, and were imprisoned, while a certain number of non juring parochial clergy were interned in Corsica, and the emperor announced his intention of reducing the number of dioceses and parishes in the Roman States by three fourths. This policy of bitter persecution coincided with fresh overtures to his prisoner, the pope, through the Austrian diplomat Lebzeltern (May, 1810). Pius VII's reply was that, to negotiate, he must be free and able to communicate with the cardinals. In July Napoleon sent Cardinals Spina and

Caselli to Savona, but they obtained nothing from the pope. There had been no solution of the internal crisis of the Church of France; while Pius VII was a prisoner the bishops were not to receive canonical institution. Bigot de Préameneu and Maury suggested to the emperor a possible arrangement; to invite the chapter in each diocese to designate the bishop who had been nominated, but not yet canonically instituted, provisional administrator. Fesch refused to lend himself to this expedient and occupy the Archbishopric of Paris; but a certain number of nominated bishops did go to their episcopal cities in the capacity of provisional administrators. Going one step further, Napoleon removed Maury from the See of Montefiascone, and d'Osmond from that of Nancy, and had them designated by the respective chapters provisional administrators of the two vacant Archdioceses of Paris and Florence. Maury and d'Osmond, at the emperor's bidding, left the dioceses given them by the pope to install themselves in these archdioceses.

Despite the rigour of his captivity, Pius VII was able to make known the pontifical commands to Cardinal di Pietro at Semur; a secret agency at Lyons, established by certain members of the Congregation, devised ingenious ways of facilitating these communications as well as the circulation of Bulls. In November, 1810, the Court was stupefied with the news that two Bulls of Pius VII, addressed to the Chapters of Florence and Paris, forbade their recognizing D'Osmond and Maury. The imperial fury was let loose. On 1 January, 1811, Napoleon, during an audience to Maury and the canons, demanded an explanation from d'Astros, the vicar capitular, who had received the Bull, telling him that there is "as much difference between the religion of Bossuet and that of Gregory VII as between heaven and hell"; d'Astros, taken by Maury himself to police headquarters, was imprisoned at Vincennes. At the Council of State, 4 January, 1811, Portalis, a relative of d'Astros, was openly accused of treason by Napoleon, and immediately put out of the council chamber (with a brutality that the emperor afterwards regretted) and was then ordered to quit Paris. Cardinals di Pietro, Oppizzone, and Gabrielli, and the priests Fontana and Gregori, former counsellors of the pope, were thrown into prison. Maury used his influence with the canons of Paris to induce them to apologize to Napoleon, who received them, told them that the pope must not treat him as a *roi fainéant*, and declared that, since the pope was not acting up to the Concordat in the matter of institution of bishops, the emperor, on his side, renounced the Concordat. The conditions of the pope's captivity were made more severe; all his correspondence had to pass through Paris, to be inspected by the Government; the lock of his desk was picked; he could no longer receive visits without the presence of witnesses; a gendarme demanded of him the ring of St. Peter, which Pius VII surrendered after breaking it in two. Chabrol, the pope's custodian, showed him the addresses to which some of the chapters were expressing their submission to the emperor, but Pius VII was inflexible. A commission of jurisconsults in Paris, after discussing the possibility of a law regulating the canonical institution of bishops without the pope's co operation, ended by deciding that to pass such a law was almost equivalent to schism.

Napoleon was not willing to go so far. He summoned the ecclesiastical council which he had already established and, 8 February, 1811, proposed to it these two questions: (1) All communication between the pope and the emperor's subjects being interrupted, to whom must recourse be had for the dispensations ordinarily granted by the Holy See? (2) What canonical means is there of providing institution for bishops when the pope reuses it? Fesch and Emery tried to sway the council towards some courses which would save the papal prerogative. But the majority of the council answered: (1) That recourse might be had, provisionally, to the bishops for the dispensations in question; 2) That a clause might be added to the Concordat stipulating that the pope must grant canonical institution within a stated time; failing which, the right of institution would devolve upon the council of the province; and that, if the pope rejected this amendment of the Corcordat, the Pragmatic Sanction would have to be revived so far as concerned bishops. The council added that, if the pope persisted in his refusal, the possibility of a public abolition of the Concordat by the emperor would have to be considered; but that these questions could be broached only by a national council, after one last attempt at negotiation with the pope.

On 16 March, 1811, Napoleon summoned to the Tuileries the members of the council and several of the great dignitaries of the empire; inveighing bitterly against the pope, he proclaimed that the Concordat no longer existed and that he was going to convoke a council of the West. At this meeting Emery, who died on 28 April, boldly faced Napoleon, quoting to him passages from Bossuet on the necessity of the pope's liberty. Pius VII not yielding to a last summons on the part of Chabrol, the council was convoked on 25 April to meet on 9 June. By this step Napoleon expected to subdue the pope to his will. In pursuance of a plan outlined by the philosopher Gerando, Archbishop Barral, and Bishops Duvoisin and Mannay were sent to Pius VII to gain him over on the question of the Bulls of institution. They were joined by the Bishop of Faenza, and arrived at Savona on 9 May. At first the pope refused to discuss the matter, not being free to communicate with his cardinals. But the bishops and Chabrol insisted, and the pope's physician added his efforts to theirs. They represented that the Church was becoming disorganized. At the end of nine days, the pope, who was neither eating nor drinking anything, being very much fatigued, consented, not to ratify, but to take as "a basis of negotiation" a note drawn up by the four bishops to the purport that, in case of persistent refusal on his part, canonical institution might be given to bishops after six months. On 20 May, at four o'clock in the morning, the bishops started for Paris with this note; at seven o'clock the pope summoned Chabrol and told him that he did not accept the note in any definitive sense, that he considered it only a sketch, and that he had made no formal promise. He also asked that a courier should be sent after the bishops to warn them of this. The courier bearing this message overtook the bishops at Turin on 24 May. Pius VII warned Chabrol that if the first note were exploited as representing an arrangement definitely accepted by the pope, he "would make a noise that should resound through the whole Christian world". Napoleon, in his blindness, resolved to do without the pope and put all his hopes in the council.

Council of 1811

The council convoked for 9 June, 1811, was not opened at Notre Dame until 17 June, the opening being postponed on account of the baptism of the King of Rome, just born of Marie Louise. Paternal pride and the seemingly assured destinies of his throne rendered Napoleon still more inflexible in regard to the pope. Only since 1905 has the truth about this council been known, thanks to Welschinger's researches. Under the Second Empire, when D'Haussonville wrote his work on the Roman Church and the First Empire (see below) Marshal Vallant had refused him all access to the archives of the council. These archives Welsinger was able to consult. Boulogne, Bishop of Troyes, in his opening sermon affirmed the solidarity of the pope and the bishops, while Fesch, as president of the council, made all its members swear obedience and fidelity to Pius VII. Upon this Napoleon gave Fesch a sound rating, on the evening of 19 June, at Saint Cloud. The emperor had packed his council in very arbitrary fashion, choosing only 42 out of 150 Italian bishops to mix with the French bishops, with a view to ecumenical effect. A private bulletin sent to the emperor, 24 June, noted that the fathers of the council themselves were generally impressed with a sense of restraint. The opposition to the emperor was very firmly led by Broglie, Bishop of Ghent, seconded by Aviau, Archbishop of Bordeaux, Dessole, Bishop of Chambéry, and Hirn, Bishop of

Tournai. The first general assembly of the council was held on 20 June. Bigot de Préameneu and Marescalchi, ministers of public worship for France and Italy, were present and read the imperial message, one draft of which had been rejected by Napoleon as too moderate. The final version displeased all the bishops who had any regard for the papal dignity. Napoleon in this document demanded that bishops should be instituted in accordance with the forms which had obtained before the Concordat, no see to be vacant for longer than three months, "more than sufficient time for appointing a new incumbent". He wished the council to present an address to him, and the committee that should prepare this address to be composed of the four prelates he had sent to Savona. The address, which was prepared in advance by Duvoisin, one of these four prelates, was an expression of assent to Napoleon's wishes. But the council decided to have on the committee besides these four prelates, some other bishops chosen by secret ballot, and among the latter figured Broglie. Broglie discussed Duvoisin's draft and had a number of changes made in it, and Fesch had some trouble in keeping the committee from at once demanding the liberation of the pope. The address, as voted, was nonsensical. It was not what Napoleon expected, and the audience which he was to have given to the members of the council on 30 June, did not take place.

Another committee was appointed by the council to inquire into the pope's views on the institution of bishops. After a conflict of ten days, Broglie secured against Duvoisin, by a vote of 8 to 4, a resolution to the effect that, in this matter, nothing must be done without the pope, and that the council ought to send him a deputation to learn what was his will. Napoleon was furious and said to Fesch and Barral: "I will dissolve the council. You are a pack of fools". Then, on second thought, he informed the council that Pius VII by way of concession, had formally promised canonical institution to the vacant bishoprics and had approved a clause enabling the metropolitans themselves in future, after six months vacancy of any see, to give canonical institution. Napoleon requested the council to issue a note to this effect and sent a deputation to thank the pope. First the committee voted as the emperor wished, then, on more mature consideration, suspecting some stratagem on the emperor's part, it recalled its vote, and, on 10 July, Hirn, Bishop of Tournai, speaking for the committee, proposed to the council that no decision be made until a deputation had been sent to the pope. Then, on the morning of 11 July, Napoleon pronounced the council dissolved. The following night Broglie, Hirn, and Boulogne were imprisoned at Vincennes. The emperor next thought of turning over the administration of the dioceses to the prefects, but presently took the advice of Maury, viz., to have all the members of the council called up, one by one, by the minister of public worship, and their personal assent to the imperial project obtained in this way. After fifteen days devoted to conversations between the minister and certain of the bishops, the emperor reconvoked the council for 5 August, and the council, by a vote of 80 to 13, passed the decree by which canonical institution was to be given within six months, either by the pope or, if he refused, by the metropolitan. The bishops who passed this decree tried to palliate their weakness by saying that they had no idea of committing an act of rebellion, but formally asked for, and hoped to obtain, the pope's assent. Napoleon believed himself victorious; he held in his hands the means of circumventing the pope and organizing without his co operation the administration of French and Italian dioceses. He had brought the Sacred College, the Dataria, the Penitentiary, and the Vatican Archives to Paris, and had spent several millions in improving the archiepiscopal palace which he meant to make the pontifical palace. He wished to remove the Hôtel Dieu, install the departments of the Roman Curia in its place, and make the quarter of Notre Dame and the Isle de Saint Louis the capital of Catholicism. But his victory was only apparent: to make the decree of the national council valid, the pope's ratification was needed, and once more the resistance of

Pius VII was to hold the emperor in check.

On 17 August Napoleon commissioned the Archbishops of Tours and Mechlin, the Patriarch of Venice, the Bishops of Evreux, Trier, Feltro, and Piacenza to go to Savona and demand of the pope his full adhesion to the decree of 5 August; the bishops were even to be precise in stating that the decree applied to episcopal sees in the former Papal States, so that, in giving his assent, Pius VII should by implication assent to the abolition of the temporal power. That Pius VII might not allege the absence of the cardinals as a reason for postponing his decisions, Napoleon sent to Savona five cardinals on whom he could rely (Roverella, Dugnani, Fabrizio Ruffo, Bayanne, and Doria) with instructions to support the bishops. The emperor's artifice was successful. On 6 September, 1811, Pius VII declared himself ready to yield, and charged Roverella to draw up a Brief approving the Decree of 5 August, and on 20 September the pope signed the Brief. But even then, the Brief as it was, was not what Napoleon wanted: Pius VII abstained from recognizing the council as a national council, he treated the Church of Rome as the mistress of all the Churches, and did not specify that the decree applied to the bishoprics of the Roman States; he also required that, when a metropolitan gave canonical institution, it should be given in the name of the pope. Napoleon did not publish the Brief. On 17 October he ordered the deputation of prelates to notify the pope that the decree applied equally to bishoprics in the Roman States. This interpretation Pius VII then formally repudiated, and announced once more that any further decision on his part would be postponed until he should have with him a suitable number of cardinals. Napoleon first wreaked his irritation on the Bishops of Ghent, Tournai, and Troyes, whom he forced to resign their sees and caused to be deported to various towns, then, on 3 December, he declared the Brief unacceptable, and charged the prelates to ask for another. Pius VII refused.

On 9 January, 1812, the prelates informed the pope, from the emperor, that, if the pope resisted any longer, the emperor would act on his own discretion in the matter of the institution of bishops. Pius VII sent a personal reply to the emperor, to the effect that he (the pope) needed a more numerous council and facility of communication with the faithful, and that he would then do, "to meet the emperor's wishes, all that was consistent with the duties of his Apostolic ministry." By way of rejoinder, Napoleon dictated to his minister of public worship, on 9 February, an extraordinarily vehement letter, addressed to the deputation of prelates. In it he refused to give Pius VII his liberty or to let the "black cardinals" go back to him; he made known that if the pope persisted in the refusal to govern the Church, they would do without the pope; and he advised the pope, in insulting terms, to abdicate. Chabrol, the prefect of Montenotte, read this letter to Pius VII, and advised him to surrender the tiara. "Never", was the pope's answer. Then on 23 February, Chabrol notified the pope, in the emperor's name, that Napoleon considered the Concordats abrogated, and that he would no longer permit the pope to interfere in any way in the canonical institution of the bishops. Pius VII answered that he would not change his attitude. Mme de Staël wrote to Henri Meister: "What a power is religion which gives strength to the weak when all that was strong has lost its strength!" The difference between the pope and the emperor naturally reacted upon the feelings of the clergy towards Napoleon, and upon the emperor's policy towards religion. From this time Napoleon refused the seminarists any exemption from military service. He made stricter the university monopoly of teaching, and Broglie, Bishop of Ghent, who, after leaving the prison of Vincennes, had continued to correspond with his clergy, was sent to the Island of Sainte Marguerite.

Last Great Wars: Concordat of Fontainebleau

At this time Napoleon was absolutely drunk with power. The French Empire had 130 departments; the Kingdom of Italy 240. The seven provinces of Illyria were subject to France. The rigour of the Continental blockade was ruining English commerce and embarrassing the European states. The tsar would have liked Napoleon, master of the West, to leave him freedom of action in Poland and Turkey; enraged at receiving no such concessions, he approached England. The French armies in Spain were exhausting their strength in a savage and ineffectual war against a ceaseless uprising of the native population; nevertheless Napoleon resolved to attack Russia also. At Dresden, from March to June, 1812, he held a congress of kings, and prepared for war. It was at Dresden, in May, 1812, that, under pretext of satisfying the demands of Francis Joseph for gentler treatment of the pope, Napoleon decided to have Pius VII removed from Savona to Fontainebleau; the fact is that he was afraid the English would attempt a *coup de main* on Savona and carry off the pope. After a journey the painful incidents of which have been related by d'Haussonville, following a manuscript in the British Museum, Pius VII reached Fontainebleau on 19 June. Equipages were placed at his disposal, he was desired to appear in public and officiate; but he refused, led a solitary life in the interior of the palace, and gave not the least indication of being ready to yield to Napoleon's demands.

Napoleon definitely declared war against the tsar on 22 June, 1812. The issue was soon seen to be dubious. The Russians devastated the whole country in advance of the French armies, and avoided pitched battles as much as possible. The victory of Borodino (7 September, 1812), an extremely bloody one, opened to Napoleon the gates of Moscow (14 September, 1812). He had expected to pass the winter there, but the conflagration brought about by the Russians forced him to retrace his steps westward, and the retreat of the "Grande Armée" so heroically covered by Marshall Ney, cost France the lives of numberless soldiers. The passage of the Beresina was glorious. As far as Lithuania, Napoleon shared the sufferings of his army, then he hastened to Paris, where he suppressed General Malet's conspiracy and prepared a new war for the year 1813. When he set out for Prussia it was his idea to extend his march beyond that country, through Asia to India, to knock over "the scaffolding of mercantile greatness raised by the English, and strike England to the heart". "After this", he declared, "it will be possible to settle everything and have done with this business of Rome and the pope. The cathedral of Paris will become that of the Catholic world. . . . If Bossuet were living now, he would have been Archbishop of Paris long ago, and the pope would still be at the Vatican, which would be much better for everybody, for then there would be no pontifical throne higher than that of Notre Dame, and Paris could not fear Rome. With such a president, I would hold a Council of Nicæa in Gaul."

But the failure of the Russian campaign upset all these dreams. The emperor's haughty attitude towards the Church was now modified. On 29 December, 1812, he wrote with his own hand an affectionate letter to the pope expressing a desire to end the quarrel. Duvoisin was sent to Fontainebleau to negotiate a Concordat. Napoleon's demands were these: the pope must swear to do nothing against the four articles; he must condemn the behaviour of the black cardinals towards the emperor; he must allow the Catholic sovereigns to chose two thirds of the cardinals, take up his residence in Paris, accept the decree of the council on the canonical institution of bishops, and agree to its application to the bishoprics of the Roman States. Pius VII spent ten days discussing the matter. On 18 January, 1813, the emperor himself came to Fontainebleau and spent many days in stormy interviews with the pope though, according to Pius VII's own statement to Count Paul Van der Vrecken, on 27 September, 1814, Napoleon committed no act of violence against the pope. On 25 January, 1813, a new Concordat was signed. In it there was no mention either of the Four Articles, or of the nomination of cardinals by the Catholic sovereigns, or of the pope's place of residence: the six suburbican dioceses were left at the pope's disposition, and he could moreover provide directly for ten bishoprics, either in France or in Italy - on all these points Napoleon made concessions. But on the other hand, the pope confirmed the decree of the Council of 1811 on the canonical institution of bishops.

According to the very words of its preamble, this Concordat was intended only "to serve as basis for a definitive arrangement". But, on 13 February, Napoleon had it published, just as it stood, as a law of the State. This was very unfair towards Pius VII: the emperor had no right to convert "preliminary articles" thus into a definitive act. On 9 February the imprisoned cardinals had been liberated by Napoleon; going to Fontainebleau, they had found Pius VII very anxious on the subject of the signature he had given, and which he regretted. With the advice of Consalvi, he prepared to retract the "preliminary articles". In his letter of 24 March to Napoleon he reproached himself for having signed these articles and disavowed the signature he had given. Napoleon had failed egregiously. He did not listen to the advice of the Comte de Narbonne, who, in a letter drafted by young Villemain, expressed the opinion that the pope ought to be set at liberty and sent back to Rome. It has been claimed that Napoleon had said to his ministers of State: "If I don't knock the head off the shoulders of some of those priests at Fontainebleau, matters will never be arranged." This is a legend; on the contrary, he ordered the minister of public worship to keep secret the letter of 24 March. Immediately, acting on his own authority, he declared the Concordat of Fontainebleau binding on the Church, and filled twelve vacant sees. On 5 April he had Cardinal di Pietro removed from Fontainebleau and threatened to do the same for Cardinal Pacca.

In the Dioceses of Ghent, Troyes, and Tournai, the chapters regarded the bishops appointed by Napoleon as intruders.

The irregular measures of the emperor only exasperated the resistance of the clergy. The Belgian clergy, warned by Count Van der Vrecken of the pope's retractation, began to agitate against the imperial policy. Meanwhile, on 25 April, 1813, Napoleon assumed command of the Army of Germany. The victories of Lutzen (2 May) and Bautzen (19 22 May) weakened the Prussian and Russian troops. But the emperor made the mistakes of accepting the mediation of Austria - only a device to gain time - and of consenting to hold the Congress of Prague (July). A letter from Pius VII, secretly carried in the face of many dangers by Van der Vrecken, warned the Congress of Prague that the pope formally rejected the articles of 25 January. Napoleon continued nevertheless to send from his headquarters with the army severe orders calculated to overcome the resistance of the Belgian clergy; on 6 August he caused the director of the seminary of Ghent to be imprisoned, and all the students to be taken to Magdeburg; on 14 August he had the canons of Tournai arrested. But his perils were increasing. Joseph had been driven out of Spain. Bernadotte, King of Sweden, one of Napoleon's own veterans, was driving the french troops out of Stralsund. Under Schwarzenberg, Blücher and Bernadotte, three armies were forming against the emperor. He had but 280,000 men against 500,000. He was victor at Dresden (27 August), but his generals were falling away on all sides. He was deserted by the Bavarian contingents in the celebrated "Battle of the Nations" at Leipzig (18 19 October), the defection of the Wurtembergers and the Saxons was the chief cause of his defeat. The victories of Hanau (30 October) and Hocheim (2 November) enabled his troops to get back to France, but the Allies were soon to enter that land.

Liberation of the Pope: End of the Empire

The liberation of the pope figured on the programme of the Allies. In vain did the emperor send the Marchesa di Brignoli to Consalvi, and Fallot de Beaumont, Archbishop of Bourges, to Pius VII, to open negotiations. In vain, on 18 January, 1814, when he learned that Murat had gone over to the Allies and occupied the Roman provinces on his own account, did he offer to restore the Papal States to Pius VII. Pius VII declared that such a restitution was an act of justice, and could not be made the subject of a treaty. Meantime, Blücher and Schwarzenberg were advancing through Burgundy. On 24 January, Lagorse, the commandant of gendarmes who had guarded Pius VII for four years, announced to him that he was about to take him back to Rome. The pope was conveyed by short stages through southern and central France. Napoleon defeated the Allies at Saint Dizier and at Brienne (27 29 January, 1814), the princes offered peace on condition that Napoleon should restore the boundaries of France to what they were in 1792. He refused. As the Allies demanded the liberation of the pope, Napoleon sent orders to Lagorse, who was taking him through the south of France, to let him make his way to Italy. On 10 March the prefect of Montenotte received orders to have the pope conducted as far as the Austrian outposts in the territory of Piacenza. The captivity of Pius VII was at an end.

The war was resumed immediately after the Congress of Chatillon. In five days Napoleon gave battle to Blücher four times at Champaubert, Montmirail, Chateau Thierry, and Vauchamp, and hurled him back on Chalons; against Schwarzenberg he fought the battles of Guiges, Mormant, Nangis, and Méry, thus opening the way to Troyes. But Lyons was taken by the Austrians, Bordeaux by the English. Exhausted as he was Napoleon beat Blücher again at Craonne (7 March), retook Reims and Epernay, and contemplated cutting off the retreat of Blücher and Schwarzenberg on the

Rhine. He caused a general levy to be decreed; but the Allies had their agents in Paris. Marmont and Mortier capitulated. On 31 March the Allies entered Paris. On 3 April the Senate declared Napoleon dethroned. Returning to Fontainebleau, the emperor, determined to try one last effort, was stopped by the defection of Marmont's corps at Essonnes. On 20 April he left Fontainebleau; on 4 May he was in Elba.

At the end of ten months, learning of the unpopularity of the regime founded in France by Louis XVIII, Napoleon secretly left Elba, landed at Cannes (1 March, 1815), and went in triumph from Grenoble to Paris (20 March, 1815). Louis VIII fled to Ghent. Then began the Hundred Days. Napoleon desired to give France liberty and religious peace forthwith. On the one hand, by the *Acte Additionnel*, he guaranteed the country a constitutional Government; on the other hand (4 April, 1815), he caused the Duke of Vicenza to write to Cardinal Pacca, and he himself wrote to Pius VII, letters in a pacific spirit, while Isoard, auditor of the Rota, was commissioned to treat with the pope in his name. But the Coalition was re formed. Napoleon had 118,000 recruits against more than 800,000 soldiers; he beat Blücher at Ligny (16 June), whilst Ney beat Wellington at Quatre Bras; next day, at Waterloo, Napoleon was victorious over Bülow and Wellington until seven o'clock in the evening, but the arrival of 30,000 Prussians, under Blücher, resulted in the emperor's defeat. He abdicated in favour of his son, set out for Rochefort, and claimed the hospitality of England. England declared him the prisoner of the Coalition and, in spite of his protests, had him taken to the Island of St. Helena. There he remained until his death, strictly watched by Hudson Lowe, and dictated to General Montholon, Gourgaud, and Bertrand those "Mémoires" which entitle him to a place among the great writers. Las Casas, at the same time, wrote day by day, the "Mémorial de Sainte Hélène", a journal of the emperor's conversations. In the first of his captivity, Napoleon complained to Montholon of having no chaplain. "It would rest my soul to hear Mass", he said. Pius VII petitioned England to accede to Napoleon's wish, and the Abbé Vignali became his chaplain. On 20 April, 1821, Napoleon said to him: "I was born in the Catholic religion. I wish to fulfil the duties it imposes, and receive the succour it administers." To Montholon he affirmed his belief in God, read aloud the Old Testament, the Gospels, and the acts of the Apostles. He spoke of Pius VII as "an old man full of tolerance and light". "Fatal circumstances," he added "embroiled our cabinets. I regret it exceedingly." Lord Rosebery has attached much importance to the paradoxes with which the emperor used to tease Gourgaud, and amused himself in maintaining the superiority of Mohammedanism, Protestantism, or Materialism. One day, when he had been talking in this strain, Montholon said to him: "I know that your Majesty does not believe one word of what you have just been saying". "You are right", said the emperor. "At any rate it helps to pass an hour."

Napoleon was not an unbeliever; but he would not admit that anyone was above himself, not even the pope. "Alexander the great", he once said to Fontanes, "declared himself the son of Jupiter. And in my time I find a priest who is more powerful than I am." This transcendent pride dictated his religious policy and utterly vitiated it. By the Concordat, as Talleyrand said, he had "done not only an act of justice, but also a very clever act, for by this one deed he had rallied to himself the sympathies of the whole Catholic world." But the same Talleyrand declares, in his "Mémoires", that his struggle with Rome was produced by "the most insensate ambition", and that when he wished to deprive the pope of the institution of bishops, "he was all the more culpable because he had had before him the errors of the Constituent Assembly". This double judgment of the former Constitutional bishop, later the emperor's minister of foreign affairs, will be accepted by posterity. By a strange destiny, this emperor who travelled all over Europe, and whose attitude towards the Catholic religion was in a measure inherited from the old Roman emperors, never set foot in Rome; through him Rome was for many years deprived of the presence of the remotest successor of St. Sylvester and of Leo III; but the successor of Constantine and of Charlemagne did not see Rome, and Rome did not see him.

A BIOGRAPHY FROM
Catholic Encyclopedia, Volume 10, 1913

BIOGRAPHICAL SKETCH

By Ida M. Tarbell

Napoleon Bonaparte was born at Ajaccio, Corsica, on August 15, 1769, the fourth child of Charles Bonaparte and Lætitia Romolino. He was educated in France at the Royal Military Schools of Brienne and of Paris, and when sixteen years old was appointed second lieutenant in a French artillery regiment. From November, 1785, to May, 1792, he was alternately with his regiment and on leaves of absence in Corsica. Sympathizing with the French Revolution, he attempted to aid the Revolutionary party in Corsica against the party of the Corsican patriot, Paoli, but was defeated, and obliged with his family to fly to France. In October, 1793, he was given command of the artillery at the siege of Toulon, and distinguished himself in the capture of the town. After a year and a half of military service in the south, he returned to Paris, and on the 13th *Vendémiaire* (October 5), 1795, he commanded the troops of the Convention against the sections. This led to his being appointed, in 1796, commander-in-chief of the Army of Italy. He went to his post in March, 1796, and after a series of successful battles drove the Austrians into Mantua. Four attempts to relieve the city were made by the enemy, but failed, and in February, 1797, Wurmser, the Austrian general, surrendered. Bonaparte then drove the rest of the Austrian force from Italy, and in October, 1797, signed the treaty of Campo Formio.

In May, 1798, he undertook the conquest of Egypt. He succeeded in entering the country and taking possession of Cairo and Alexandria, but on August 1, at the Battle of the Nile, the French fleet was destroyed by the English under Nelson. A disastrous expedition into Syria occupied the spring of 1799. On returning to Egypt, Bonaparte received news of political disturbances in France, and leaving the army under Kléber he went to Paris, where, by *the coup d' état* of the 18th and 19th *Brumaire* (November 9 and 10) he became First Consul. During Bonaparte's absence in Egypt, war had again broken out between France and Austria, and the First Consul hurried against the enemy. The Battle of Marengo on June 14, 1800, again drove the Austrians from Italy, and February, 1801, peace was concluded. A treaty with England followed in March, 1802. Napoleon now took hold of the reorganization of France with great energy, but in May, 1803, war again broke out between France and England, and the First Consul made elaborate preparations to invade England. While preparing for invasion he was crowned Emperor of the French on December 2, 1804. Before the plan against England could be carried out, Russia and Austria began hostilities, but the alliance was broken by the victory won by Napoleon at Austerlitz on December 2, 1805, and peace was signed at Presburg. The next year, 1806, there was war with Prussia and Russia. Napoleon won the Battle of Jena, October 14, entered Berlin, October 25, and issued the Berlin Decrees declaring a continental blockade against England on November 21. On February 8, 1807, he fought with the Russians the doubtful Battle of Eylau, and on June 14, the decisive Battle of Friedland. The Peace of Tilsit followed, on July 7. In 1808 Napoleon attempted to take possession of Spain, but before the conquest was complete Austria declared war. The campaign of Wagram in the spring and summer of 1809 subdued the Austrians. In December of 1809, Napoleon divorced Josephine, by whom he had ceased to hope to have an heir to the throne, and in April, 1810, he married the Austrian Princess, Marie Louise. The next year a son, the King of Rome, was born to them. The alliance between France and Russia was broken in 1812, and Napoleon invaded Russia. The campaign ended in a frightful retreat, the army being practically destroyed. Napoleon hastened to Paris, and by the spring of 1813 had a new force in the field. After successful battles at Lützen, Bautzen, and Dresden, he was routed completely at Leipsic in October. The allies invaded France in January, 1814, and a three months' campaign compelled Paris to capitulate, and Napoleon to abdicate. The treaty with the allies gave the Emperor the island of Elbe for life, and hither he went at once, but in February, 1815, he left the island for France, and was greeted joyfully by the French army and nation. Louis XVIII. was obliged to fly from the country, and Napoleon was restored to the throne. The allies immediately attacked him, and at Waterloo, on June 18, 1815, he was defeated. He again resigned the throne, and on July 15 surrendered to the English, who sent him a captive to St. Helena, where he died on May 5, 1821. Napoleon was buried on the island, but in 1840 his remains were removed to France, and placed in the Invalides.

A Chapter from
Napoleon's Addresses - Selections from the Proclamations,
Speeches and Correspondence of Napoleon Bonaparte, 1897

NAPOLEON — MAN OF THE WORLD

By Ralph Waldo Emerson

Among the eminent persons of the nineteenth century, Bonaparte is far the best known and the most powerful; and owes his predominance to the fidelity with which he expresses the tone of thought and belief, the aims of the masses of active and cultivated men. It is Swedenborg's theory that every organ is made up of homogeneous particles; or as it is sometimes expressed, every whole is made of similars; that is, the lungs are composed of infinitely small lungs; the liver, of infinitely small livers; the kidney, of little kidneys, etc. Following this analogy, if any man is found to carry with him the power and affections of vast numbers, if Napoleon is France, if Napoleon is Europe, it is because the people whom he sways are little Napoleons.

In our society there is a standing antagonism between the conservative and the democratic classes; between those who have made their fortunes, and the young and the poor who have fortunes to make; between the interests of dead labor,- that is, the labor of hands long ago still in the grave, which labor is now entombed in money stocks, or in land and buildings owned by idle capitalists,- and the interests of living labor, which seeks to possess itself of land and buildings and money stocks. The first class is timid, selfish, illiberal, hating innovation, and continually losing numbers by death. The second class is selfish also, encroaching, bold, self-relying, always outnumbering the other and recruiting its numbers every hour by births. It desires to keep open every avenue to the competition of all, and to multiply avenues: the class of business men in America, in

England, in France and throughout Europe; the class of industry and skill. Napoleon is its representative. The instinct of active, brave, able men, throughout the middle class everywhere, has pointed out Napoleon as the incarnate Democrat. He had their virtues and their vices; above all, he had their spirit or aim. That tendency is material, pointing at a sensual success and employing the richest and most various means to that end; conversant with mechanical powers, highly intellectual, widely and accurately learned and skilful, but subordinating all intellectual and spiritual forces into means to a material success. To be the rich man, is the end. "God has granted," says the Koran, "to every people a prophet in its own tongue." Paris and London and New York, the spirit of commerce, of money and material power, were also to have their prophet; and Bonaparte was qualified and sent.

Every one of the million readers of anecdotes or memoirs or lives of Napoleon, delights in the page, because he studies in it his own history. Napoleon is thoroughly modern, and, at the highest point of his fortunes, has the very spirit of the newspapers. He is no saint,- to use his own word, "no capuchin," and he is no hero, in the high sense. The man in the street finds in him the qualities and powers of other men in the street. He finds him, like himself, by birth a citizen, who, by very intelligible merits, arrived at such a commanding position that he could indulge all those tastes which the common man possesses but is obliged to conceal and deny: good society, good books, fast travelling, dress, dinners, servants without number, personal weight, the execution of his ideas, the standing in the attitude of a benefactor to all persons about him, the refined enjoyments of pictures, statues, music, palaces and conventional honors,- precisely what is agreeable to the heart of every man in the nineteenth century, this powerful man possessed.

It is true that a man of Napoleon's truth of adaptation to the mind of the masses around him, becomes not merely representative but actually a monopolizer and usurper of other minds. Thus Mirabeau plagiarized every good thought, every good word that was spoken in France. Dumont relates that he sat in the gallery of the Convention and heard Mirabeau make a speech. It struck Dumont that he could fit it with a peroration, which he wrote in pencil immediately, and showed it to Lord Elgin, who sat by him. Lord Elgin approved it, and Dumont, in the evening, showed it to Mirabeau. Mirabeau read it, pronounced it admirable, and declared he would incorporate it into his harangue to-morrow, to the Assembly. "It is impossible," said Dumont, "as, unfortunately, I have shown it to Lord Elgin." "If you have shown it to Lord Elgin and to fifty persons beside, I shall still speak it to-morrow": and he did speak it, with much effect, at the next day's session. For Mirabeau, with his overpowering personality, felt that these things which his presence inspired were as much his own as if he had said them, and that his adoption of them gave them their weight. Much more absolute and centralizing was the successor to Mirabeau's popularity and to much more than his predominance in France. Indeed, a man of Napoleon's stamp almost ceases to have a private speech and opinion. He is so largely receptive, and is so placed, that he comes to be a bureau for all the intelligence, wit and power of the age and country. He gains the battle; he makes the code; he makes the system of weights and measures; he levels the Alps; he builds the road. All distinguished engineers, savans, statists, report to him: so likewise do all good heads in every kind: he adopts the best measures, sets his stamp on them, and not these alone, but on every happy and memorable expression. Every sentence spoken by Napoleon and every line of his writing, deserves reading, as it is the sense of France.

Bonaparte was the idol of common men because he had in transcendent degree the qualities and powers of common men. There is a certain satisfaction in coming down to the lowest ground of politics, for we get rid of cant and hypocrisy. Bonaparte wrought, in common with that great class he represented, for power and wealth,- but Bonaparte, specially, without any scruple as to the means. All the sentiments which embarrass men's pursuit of these objects, he set aside. The sentiments were for women and children. Fontanes, in 1804, expressed Napoleon's own sense, when in behalf of the Senate he addressed him,- "Sire, the desire of perfection is the worst disease that ever afflicted the human mind." The advocates of liberty and of progress are "ideologists";- a word of contempt often in his mouth;- "Necker is an ideologist": "Lafayette is an ideologist."

An Italian proverb, too well known, declares that "if you would succeed, you must not be too good." It is an advantage, within certain limits, to have renounced the dominion of the sentiments of piety, gratitude and generosity; since what was an impassable bar to us, and still is to others, becomes a convenient weapon for our purposes; just as the river which was a formidable barrier, winter transforms into the smoothest of roads.

Napoleon renounced, once for all, sentiments and affections, and would help himself with his hands and his head. With him is no miracle and no magic. He is a worker in brass, in iron, in wood, in earth, in roads, in buildings, in money and in troops, and a very consistent and wise master-workman. He is never weak and literary, but acts with the solidity and the precision of natural agents. He has not lost his native sense and sympathy with things. Men give way before such a man, as before natural events. To be sure there are men enough who are immersed in things, as farmers, smiths, sailors and mechanics generally; and we know how real and solid such men appear in the presence of scholars and grammarians: but these men ordinarily lack the power of arrangement, and are like hands without a head. But Bonaparte superadded to this mineral and animal force, insight and generalization, so that men saw in him combined the natural and the intellectual power, as if the sea and land had taken flesh and begun to cipher. Therefore the land and sea seem to presuppose him. He came unto his own and they received him. This ciphering operative knows what he is working with and what is the product. He knew the properties of gold and iron, of wheels and ships, of troops and diplomatists, and required that each should do after its kind.

The art of war was the game in which he exerted his arithmetic. It consisted, according to him, in having always more forces than the enemy, on the point where the enemy is attacked, or where he attacks: and his whole talent is strained by endless manoeuvre and evolution, to march always on the enemy at an angle, and destroy his forces in detail. It is obvious that a very small force, skilfully and rapidly manoeuvring so as always to bring two men against one at the point of engagement, will be an overmatch for a much larger body of men.

The times, his constitution and his early circumstances combined to develop this pattern democrat. He had the virtues of his class and the conditions for their activity. That common-sense which no sooner respects any end than it finds the means to effect it; the delight in the use of means; in the choice, simplification and combining of means; the directness and thoroughness of his work; the prudence with which all was seen and the energy with which all was done, make him the natural organ and head of what I may almost call, from its extent, the modern party.

Nature must have far the greatest share in every success, and so in his. Such a man was wanted, and such a man was born; a man of stone and iron, capable of sitting on horseback sixteen or seventeen hours, of going many days together without rest or food except by snatches, and with the speed and spring of a tiger in action; a man not embarrassed by any scruples; compact, instant, selfish, prudent, and of a perception which did not suffer itself to be baulked or misled by any pretences of others, or any superstition or any heat or haste of his own. "My hand of iron," he said, "was not at the extremity of my arm, it was immediately connected with my head." He respected the power of nature and fortune, and ascribed to it his superiority, instead of valuing himself, like inferior men, on his opinionativeness, and waging war with nature. His favorite rhetoric lay in allusion to his star; and he pleased himself, as well as the people, when he styled himself the "Child of Destiny." "They charge me," he said, "with the commission of great crimes: men of my stamp do not commit crimes. Nothing has been more simple than my elevation, 'tis in vain to ascribe it to intrigue or crime; it was owing to the peculiarity of the times and to my reputation of having fought well against the enemies of my country. I have always marched with the opinion of great masses and with events. Of what use then would crimes be to me?" Again he said, speaking of his son, "My son can not replace me; I could not replace myself. I am the creature of circumstances."

He had a directness of action never before combined with so much comprehension. He is a realist, terrific to all talkers and confused truth-obscuring persons. He sees where the matter hinges, throws himself on the precise point of resistance, and slights all other considerations. He is strong in the right manner, namely by insight. He never blundered into victory, but won his battles in his head before he won them on the field. His principal means are in himself. He asks counsel of no other. In 1796 he writes to the Directory: "I have conducted the campaign without consulting any one. I should have done no good if I had been under the necessity of conforming to the notions of another person. I have gained some advantages over superior forces and when totally destitute of every thing, because, in the persuasion that your confidence was reposed in me, my actions were as prompt as my thoughts."

History is full, down to this day, of the imbecility of kings and governors. They are a class of persons much to be pitied, for they know not what they should do. The weavers strike for bread, and the king and his ministers, knowing not what to do, meet them with bayonets. But Napoleon understood his business. Here was a man who in each moment and emergency knew what to do next. It is an immense comfort and refreshment to the spirits, not only of kings, but of citizens. Few men have any next; they live from hand to mouth, without plan, and are ever at the end of their line, and after each action wait for an impulse from abroad. Napoleon had been the first man of the world, if his ends had been purely public. As he is, he inspires confidence and vigor by the extraordinary unity of his action. He is firm, sure, self-denying, self-postponing, sacrificing every thing,- money, troops, generals, and his own safety also, to his aim; not misled, like common adventurers, by the splendor of his own means. "Incidents ought not to govern policy," he said, "but policy, incidents." "To be hurried away by every event is to have no political system at all." His victories were only so many doors, and he never for a moment lost sight of his way onward, in the dazzle and uproar of the present circumstance. He knew what to do, and he flew to his mark. He would shorten a straight line to come at his object. Horrible anecdotes may no doubt be collected from his history, of the price at which he bought his successes; but he must not therefore be set down as cruel, but only as one who knew no impediment to his will; not bloodthirsty, not cruel,- but woe to what thing or person stood in his way! Not bloodthirsty, but not sparing of blood,- and pitiless. He saw only the object: the obstacle must give way. "Sire, General Clarke can not combine with General Junot, for the dreadful fire of the Austrian battery."- "Let him carry the battery."- "Sire, every regiment that approaches the heavy artillery is sacrificed: Sire, what orders?"- "Forward, forward!" Seruzier, a colonel of artillery, gives, in his "Military Memoirs," the following sketch of a scene after the battle of Austerlitz.- "At the moment in which the Russian army was making its retreat, painfully, but in good order, on the ice of the lake, the Emperor Napoleon came riding at full speed toward the artillery. 'You are losing time,' he cried; 'fire upon those masses; they must be engulfed: fire upon the ice!' The order remained unexecuted for ten minutes. In vain several officers and myself were placed on the slope of a hill to produce the effect: their balls and mine rolled upon the ice without breaking it up. Seeing that, I tried a simple method of elevating light howitzers. The almost perpendicular fall of the heavy projectiles produced the desired effect. My method was immediately followed by the adjoining batteries, and in less than no time we buried" some "thousands of Russians and Austrians under the waters of the lake."

In the plenitude of his resources, every obstacle seemed to vanish. "There shall be no Alps," he said; and he built his perfect roads, climbing by graded galleries their steepest precipices, until Italy was as open to Paris as any town in France. He laid his bones to, and wrought for his crown. Having decided what was to be done, he did that with might and main. He put out all his strength. He risked every thing and spared nothing, neither ammunition, nor money, nor troops, nor generals, nor himself.

We like to see every thing do its office after its kind, whether it be a milch-cow or a rattlesnake; and if fighting be the best mode of adjusting national differences, (as large majorities of men seem to agree,) certainly Bonaparte was right in making it thorough. The grand principle of war, he said, was that an army ought always to be ready, by day and by night and at all hours, to make all the resistance it is capable of making. He never economized his ammunition, but, on a hostile position, rained a torrent of iron,- shells, balls, grape-shot,- to annihilate all defence. On any point of resistance he concentrated squadron on squadron in overwhelming numbers until it was swept out of existence. To a regiment of horse-chasseurs at Lobenstein, two days before the battle of Jena, Napoleon said, "My lads, you must not fear death; when soldiers brave death, they drive him into the enemy's ranks." In the fury of assault, he no more spared himself. He went to the edge of his possibility. It is plain that in Italy he did what he could, and all that he could. He came, several times, within an inch of ruin; and his own person was all but lost. He was flung into the marsh at Arcola. The Austrians were between him and his troops, in the melee, and he was brought off with desperate efforts. At Lonato, and at other places, he was on the point of being taken prisoner. He fought sixty battles. He had never enough. Each victory was a new weapon. "My power would fall, were I not to support it by new achievements. Conquest has made me what I am, and conquest must maintain me." He felt, with every wise man, that as much life is needed for conservation as for creation. We are always in peril, always in a bad plight, just on the edge of destruction and only to be saved by invention and courage.

This vigor was guarded and tempered by the coldest prudence and punctuality. A thunderbolt in the attack, he was found invulnerable in his intrenchments. His very attack was never the inspiration of courage, but the result of calculation. His idea of the best defence consists in being still the attacking party. "My ambition," he says, "was great, but was of a cold nature." In one of his conversations with Las Cases, he remarked, "As to moral courage, I have rarely met with the two-o'clock-in-the-morning kind: I mean unprepared courage; that which is necessary on an unexpected occasion, and which, in spite of the most unforeseen events, leaves full freedom of judgment and decision": and he did not hesitate to declare that he was himself eminently endowed with this two-o'clock-in-the-morning courage, and that he had met with few persons equal to himself in this respect.

Every thing depended on the nicety of his combinations, and the stars were not more punctual than his arithmetic. His personal attention descended to the smallest particulars. "At Montebello, I ordered Kellermann to attack with eight hundred horse, and with these he separated the six thousand Hungarian grenadiers, before the very eyes of the Austrian cavalry. This cavalry was half a league off and required a quarter of an hour to arrive on the field of action, and I have observed that it is always these quarters of an hour that decide the fate of a battle." "Before he fought a battle, Bonaparte thought little about what he should do in case of success, but a great deal about what he should do in case of a reverse of fortune." The same prudence and good sense mark all his behavior. His instructions to his secretary at the Tuileries are worth remembering. "During the night, enter my chamber as seldom as possible. Do not awake me when you have any good news to communicate; with that there is no hurry. But when you bring bad news, rouse me instantly, for then there is not a moment to be lost." It was a whimsical economy of the same kind which dictated his practice, when general in Italy, in regard to his burdensome correspondence. He directed Bourrienne to leave all letters unopened for three weeks, and then observed with satisfaction how large a part of the correspondence had thus disposed of itself and no longer required an answer. His achievement of business was immense, and enlarges the known powers of man. There have been many working kings, from Ulysses to William of Orange, but none who accomplished a tithe of this man's performance.

To these gifts of nature, Napoleon added the advantage of having been born to a private and humble fortune. In his later days he had the weakness of wishing to add to his crowns and badges the prescription of aristocracy; but he knew his debt to his austere education, and made no secret of his contempt for the born kings, and for "the hereditary asses," as he coarsely styled the Bourbons. He said that "in their exile they had learned nothing, and forgot nothing." Bonaparte had passed through all the degrees of military service, but also was citizen before he was emperor, and so has the key to citizenship. His remarks and estimates discover the information and justness of measurement of the middle class. Those who had to deal with him found that he was not to be imposed upon, but could cipher as well as another man. This appears in all parts of his Memoirs, dictated at St. Helena. When the expenses of the empress, of his household, of his palaces, had accumulated great debts, Napoleon examined the bills of the creditors himself, detected overcharges and errors, and reduced the claims by considerable sums.

His grand weapon, namely the millions whom he directed, he owed to the representative character which clothed him. He interests us as he stands for France and for Europe; and he exists as captain and king only as far as the Revolution, or the interest of the industrious masses, found an organ and a leader in him. In the social interests, he knew the meaning and value of labor, and threw himself naturally on that side. I like an incident mentioned by one of his biographers at St. Helena. "When walking with Mrs. Balcombe, some servants, carrying heavy boxes, passed by on the road, and Mrs. Balcombe desired them, in rather an angry tone, to keep back. Napoleon interfered, saying 'Respect the burden, Madam.'" In the time of the empire he directed attention to the improvement and embellishment of the markets of the capital. "The market-place," he said, "is the Louvre of the common people." The principal works that have survived him are his magnificent roads. He filled the troops with his spirit, and a sort of freedom and companionship grew up between him and them, which the forms of his court never permitted between the officers and himself. They performed, under his eye, that which no others could do. The best document of his relation to his troops is the order of the day on the morning of the battle of Austerlitz, in which Napoleon promises the troops that he will keep his person out of reach of fire. This declaration, which is the reverse of that ordinarily made by generals and sovereigns on the eve of a battle, sufficiently explains the devotion of the army to their leader.

But though there is in particulars this identity between Napoleon and the mass of the people, his real strength lay in their conviction that he was their representative in his genius and aims, not only when he courted, but when he controlled, and even when he decimated them by his conscriptions. He knew, as well as any Jacobin in France, how to philosophize on liberty and equality; and when allusion was made to the precious blood of centuries, which was spilled by the killing of the Duc d'Enghien, he suggested, "Neither is my blood ditchwater." The people felt that no longer the throne was occupied and the land sucked of its nourishment, by a small class of legitimates, secluded from all community with the children of the soil, and holding the ideas and superstitions of a long-forgotten state of society. Instead of that vampyre, a man of themselves held, in the Tuileries, knowledge and ideas like their own, opening of course to them and their children all places of power and trust. The day of sleepy, selfish policy, ever narrowing the means and opportunities of young men, was ended, and a day of expansion and demand was come. A market for all the powers and productions of man was opened; brilliant prizes glittered in the eyes of youth and talent. The old, iron-bound, feudal France was changed into a young Ohio or New York; and those who smarted under the immediate rigors of the new monarch, pardoned them as the necessary severities of the military system which had driven out the oppressor. And even when the majority of the people had begun to ask whether they had really gained any thing under the exhausting levies of men and money of the new master, the whole talent of the country, in every rank and kindred, took his part and defended him as its natural patron. In 1814, when advised to rely on the higher classes, Napoleon said to those around him, "Gentlemen, in the situation in which I stand, my only nobility is the rabble of the Faubourgs."

Napoleon met this natural expectation. The necessity of his position required a hospitality to every sort of talent, and its appointment to trusts; and his feeling went along with this policy. Like every superior person, he undoubtedly felt a desire for men and compeers, and a wish to measure his power with other masters, and an impatience of fools and underlings. In Italy, he sought for men and found none. "Good God!" he said, "how rare men are! There are eighteen millions in Italy, and I have with difficulty found two,- Dandolo and Melzi." In later years, with larger experience, his respect for mankind was not increased. In a moment of bitterness he said to one of his oldest friends, "Men deserve the contempt with which they inspire me. I have only to put some gold-lace on the coat of my virtuous republicans and they immediately become just what I wish them." This impatience at levity was, however, an oblique tribute of respect to those able persons who commanded his regard not only when he found them friends and coadjutors but also when they resisted his will. He could not confound Fox and Pitt, Carnot, Lafayette and Bernadotte, with the danglers of his court; and in spite of the detraction which his systematic egotism dictated toward the great captains who conquered with and for him, ample acknowledgments are made by him to Lannes, Duroc, Kleber, Dessaix, Massena, Murat, Ney and Augereau. If he felt himself their patron and the founder of their fortunes, as when he said, "I made my generals out of mud,"- he could not hide his satisfaction in receiving from them a seconding and support commensurate with the grandeur of his enterprise. In the Russian campaign he was so much impressed by the courage and resources of Marshal Ney, that he said, "I have two hundred millions in my coffers, and I would give them all for Ney." The characters which he has drawn of several of his marshals are discriminating, and though they did not content the insatiable vanity of French officers, are no doubt substantially just. And in fact every species of merit was sought and advanced under his government. "I know," he said, "the depth and draught of water of every one of my generals." Natural power was sure to be well received at his court. Seventeen men in his time were raised from common soldiers to the rank of king, marshal, duke, or general; and the crosses of his Legion of Honor were given to personal valor, and not to family connexion. "When soldiers have been baptized in the fire of a battlefield, they have all one rank in my eyes."

When a natural king becomes a titular king, every body is pleased and satisfied. The Revolution entitled the strong populace of the Faubourg St. Antoine, and every horse-boy and powder-monkey in the army, to look on Napoleon as flesh of his flesh and the creature of his party: but there is something in the success of grand talent which enlists an universal sympathy. For in the prevalence of sense and spirit over stupidity and malversation, all reasonable men have an interest; and as intellectual beings we feel the air purified by the electric shock, when material force is overthrown by intellectual energies. As soon as we are removed out of the reach of local and accidental partialities, Man feels that Napoleon fights for him; these are honest victories; this strong steam-engine does our work. Whatever appeals to the imagination, by transcending the ordinary limits of human ability, wonderfully encourages us and liberates us. This capacious head, revolving and disposing sovereignly trains of affairs, and animating such multitudes of agents; this eye, which looked through Europe; this prompt invention; this inexhaustible resource:- what events! what romantic pictures! what strange situations!- when spying the Alps, by a sunset in the Sicilian sea; drawing up his army for battle in sight of the Pyramids, and saying to his troops, "From the tops of those pyramids, forty centuries look down on you"; fording the Red Sea; wading in the gulf of the Isthmus of Suez. On the shore of Ptolemais, gigantic projects agitated him. "Had Acre fallen, I should have changed the face of the world." His army, on the night of the battle of Austerlitz, which was the anniversary of his inauguration as Emperor, presented him with a bouquet of forty standards taken in the fight. Perhaps it is a little puerile, the pleasure he took in making these contrasts glaring; as when he pleased himself with making kings wait in his antechambers, at Tilsit, at Paris and at Erfurt.

We can not, in the universal imbecility, indecision and indolence of men, sufficiently congratulate ourselves on this strong and ready actor, who took occasion by the beard, and showed us how much may be accomplished by the mere force of such virtues as all men possess in less degrees; namely, by punctuality, by personal attention, by courage and thoroughness. "The Austrians," he said, "do not know the value of time." I should cite him, in his earlier years, as a model of prudence. His power does not consist in any wild or extravagant force; in any enthusiasm like Mahomet's, or singular power of persuasion; but in the exercise of common-sense on each emergency, instead of abiding by rules and customs. The lesson he teaches is that which vigor always teaches;- that there is always room for it. To what heaps of cowardly doubts is not that man's life an answer. When he appeared it was the belief of all military men that there could be nothing new in war; as it is the belief of men to-day that nothing new can be undertaken in politics, or in church, or in letters, or in trade, or in farming, or in our social manners and customs; and as it is at all times the belief of society that the world is used up. But Bonaparte knew better than society; and moreover knew that he knew better. I think all men know better than they do; know that the institutions we so volubly commend are go-carts and baubles; but they dare not trust their presentiments. Bonaparte relied on his own sense, and did not care a bean for other people's. The world treated his novelties just as it treats everybody's novelties,- made infinite objection, mustered all the impediments; but he snapped his finger at their objections. "What creates great difficulty," he remarks, "in the profession of the land-commander, is the necessity of feeding so many men and animals. If he allows himself to be guided by the commissaries he will never stir, and all his expeditions will fail." An example of his common-sense is what he says of the passage of the Alps in winter, which all writers, one repeating after the other, had described as impracticable. "The winter," says Napoleon, "is not the most unfavorable season for the passage of lofty mountains. The snow is then firm, the weather settled, and there is nothing to fear from avalanches, the real and only danger to be apprehended in the Alps. On these high mountains there are often very fine days in December, of a dry cold, with extreme calmness in the air." Read his account, too, of the way in which battles are gained. "In all battles a moment occurs when the bravest troops, after having made the greatest efforts, feel inclined to run. That terror proceeds from a want of confidence in their own courage, and it only requires a slight opportunity, a pretence, to restore confidence to them. The art is, to give rise to the opportunity and to invent the pretence. At Arcola I won the battle with twenty-five horsemen. I seized that moment of lassitude, gave every man a trumpet, and gained the day with this handful. You see that two armies are two bodies which meet and endeavor to frighten each other; a moment of panic occurs, and that moment must be turned to advantage. When a man has been present in many actions, he distinguishes that moment without difficulty: it is as easy as casting up an addition."

This deputy of the nineteenth century added to his gifts a capacity for speculation on general topics. He delighted in running through the range of practical, of literary and of abstract questions. His opinion is always original and to the purpose. On the voyage to Egypt he liked, after dinner, to fix on three or four persons to support a proposition, and as many to oppose it. He gave a subject, and the discussions turned on questions of religion, the different kinds of government, and the art of war. One day he asked whether the planets were inhabited? On another, what was the age of the world? Then he proposed to consider the probability of the destruction of the globe, either by water or by fire: at another time, the truth or fallacy of presentiments, and the interpretation of dreams. He was very fond of talking of religion. In 1806 he conversed with Fournier, bishop of Montpellier, on matters of theology. There were two points on which they could not agree, viz. that of hell, and that of salvation out of the pale of the church. The Emperor told Josephine that he disputed like a devil on these two points, on which the bishop was inexorable. To the philosophers he readily yielded all that was proved against religion as the work of men and time, but he would not hear of materialism. One fine night, on deck, amid a clatter of materialism, Bonaparte pointed to the stars, and said, "You may talk as long as you please, gentlemen, but who made all that?" He delighted in the conversation of men of science, particularly of Monge and Berthollet; but the men of letters he slighted; they were "manufacturers of phrases." Of medicine too he was fond of talking, and with those of its practitioners whom he most esteemed,- with Corvisart at Paris, and with Antonomarchi at St. Helena. "Believe me," he said to the last, "we had better leave off all these remedies: life is a fortress which neither you nor I know any thing about. Why throw obstacles in the way of its defence? Its own means are superior to all the apparatus of your laboratories. Corvisart candidly agreed with me that all your filthy mixtures are good for nothing. Medicine is a collection of uncertain prescriptions, the results of which, taken collectively, are more fatal than useful to mankind. Water, air and cleanliness are the chief articles in my pharmacopoeia."

His memoirs, dictated to Count Montholon and General Gourgaud at St. Helena, have great value, after all the deduction that it seems is to be made from them on account of his known disingenuousness. He has the good-nature of strength and conscious superiority. I admire his simple, clear narrative of his battles;- good as Caesar's; his good-natured and sufficiently respectful account of Marshal Wurmser and his other antagonists; and his own equality as a writer to his varying subject. The most agreeable portion is the Campaign in Egypt.

He had hours of thought and wisdom. In intervals of leisure, either in the camp or the palace, Napoleon appears as a man of genius directing on abstract questions the native appetite for truth and the impatience of words he was wont to show in war. He could enjoy every play of invention, a romance, a bon mot, as well as a strategem in a campaign. He delighted to fascinate Josephine and her ladies, in a dim-lighted apartment, by the terrors of a fiction to which his voice and dramatic power lent every addition.

I call Napoleon the agent or attorney of the middle class of modern society; of the throng who fill the markets, shops, counting-houses, manufactories, ships, of the modern world, aiming to be rich. He was the agitator, the destroyer of prescription, the internal improver, the liberal, the radical, the inventor of means, the opener of doors and markets, the subverter of monopoly and abuse. Of course the rich and aristocratic did not like him. England, the centre of capital, and Rome and Austria, centres of tradition and genealogy, opposed him. The consternation of the dull and conservative classes, the terror of the foolish old men and old women of the Roman conclave, who in their despair took hold of any thing, and would cling to red-hot iron,- the vain attempts of statists to amuse and deceive him, of the emperor of Austria to bribe him; and the instinct of the young, ardent and active men every where, which pointed him out as the giant of the middle class, make his history bright and commanding. He had the virtues of the masses of his constituents: he had also their vices. I am sorry that the brilliant picture has its reverse. But that is the fatal quality which we discover in our pursuit of wealth, that it is treacherous, and is bought by the breaking or weakening of the sentiments; and it is inevitable that we should find the same fact in the history of this champion, who proposed to himself simply a brilliant career, without any stipulation or scruple concerning the means.

Bonaparte was singularly destitute of generous sentiments. The highest-placed individual in the most cultivated age and population of the world,- he has not the merit of common truth and honesty. He is unjust to his generals; egotistic and monopolizing; meanly stealing the credit of their great actions from Kellermann, from Bernadotte; intriguing to involve his faithful Junot in hopeless bankruptcy, in order to drive him to a distance from Paris, because the familiarity of his manners offends the new pride of his throne. He is a boundless liar. The official paper, his "Moniteur," and all his bulletins, are proverbs for saying what he wished to be believed; and worse,- he sat, in his premature old age, in his lonely island, coldly falsifying facts and dates and characters, and giving to history a theatrical eclat. Like all Frenchmen he has a passion for stage effect. Every action that breathes of generosity is poisoned by this calculation. His star, his love of glory, his doctrine of the immortality of the soul, are all French. "I must dazzle and astonish. If I were to give the liberty of the press, my power could not last three days." To make a great noise is his favorite design. "A great reputation is a great noise: the more there is made, the farther off it is heard. Laws, institutions, monuments, nations, all fall; but the noise continues, and resounds in after ages." His doctrine of immortality is simply fame. His theory of influence is not flattering. "There are two levers for moving men,- interest and fear. Love is a silly infatuation, depend upon it. Friendship is but a name. I love nobody. I do not even love my brothers: perhaps Joseph a little, from habit, and because he is my elder; and Duroc, I love him too; but why?- because his character pleases me: he is stern and resolute, and I believe the fellow never shed a tear. For my part I know very well that I have no true friends. As long as I continue to be what I am, I may have as many pretended friends as I please. Leave sensibility to women; but men should be firm in heart and purpose, or they should have nothing to do with war and government." He was thoroughly unscrupulous. He would steal, slander, assassinate, drown and poison, as his interest dictated. He had no generosity, but mere vulgar hatred; he was intensely selfish; he was perfidious; he cheated at cards; he was a prodigious gossip, and opened letters, and delighted in his infamous police, and rubbed his hands with joy when he had intercepted some morsel of intelligence concerning the men and women about him, boasting that "he knew every thing"; and interfered with the cutting the dresses of the women; and listened after the hurrahs and the compliments of the street, incognito. His manners were coarse. He treated women with low familiarity. He had the habit of pulling their ears and pinching their cheeks when he was in good humor, and of pulling the ears and whiskers of men, and of striking and horse-play with them, to his last days. It does not appear that he listened at key-holes, or at least that he was caught at it. In short, when you have penetrated through all the circles of power and splendor, you were not dealing with a gentleman, at last; but with an impostor and a rogue; and he fully deserves the epithet of Jupiter Scapin, or a sort of Scamp Jupiter.

In describing the two parties into which modern society divides itself,- the democrat and the conservative,- I said, Bonaparte represents the democrat, or the party of men of business, against the stationary or conservative party. I omitted then to say, what is material to the statement, namely that these two parties differ only as young and old. The democrat is a young conservative; the conservative is an old democrat. The aristocrat is the democrat ripe and gone to seed;- because both parties stand on the one ground of the supreme value of property, which one endeavors to get, and the other to keep. Bonaparte may be said to represent the whole history of this party, its youth and its age; yes, and with poetic justice its fate, in his own. The counter-revolution, the counter-party, still waits for its organ and representative, in a lover and a man of truly public and universal aims.

Here was an experiment, under the most favorable conditions, of the powers of intellect without conscience. Never was such a leader so endowed and so weaponed; never leader found such aids and followers. And what was the result of this vast talent and power, of these immense armies, burned cities, squandered treasures, immolated millions of men, of this demoralized Europe? It came to no result. All passed away like the smoke of his artillery, and left no trace. He left France smaller, poorer, feebler, than he found it; and the whole contest for freedom was to be begun again. The attempt was in principle suicidal. France served him with life and limb and estate, as long as it could identify its interest with him; but when men saw that after victory was another war; after the destruction of armies, new conscriptions; and they who had toiled so desperately were never nearer to the reward,- they could not spend what they had earned, nor repose on their down-beds, nor strut in their chateaux,- they deserted him. Men found that his absorbing egotism was deadly to all other men. It resembled the torpedo, which inflicts a succession of shocks on any one who takes hold of it, producing spasms which contract the muscles of the hand, so that the man can not open his fingers; and the animal inflicts new and more violent shocks, until he paralyzes and kills his victim. So this exorbitant egotist narrowed, impoverished and absorbed the power and existence of those who served him; and the universal cry of France and of Europe in 1814 was, "Enough of him"; "Assez de Bonaparte."

It was not Bonaparte's fault. He did all that in him lay to live and thrive without moral principle. It was the nature of things, the eternal law of man and of the world which baulked and ruined him; and the result, in a million experiments, will be the same. Every experiment, by multitudes or by individuals, that has a sensual and selfish aim, will fail. The pacific Fourier will be as inefficient as the pernicious Napoleon. As long as our civilization is essentially one of property, of fences, of exclusiveness, it will be mocked by delusions. Our riches will leave us sick; there will be bitterness in our laughter, and our wine will burn our mouth. Only that good profits which we can taste with all doors open, and which serves all men.

A CHAPTER FROM
Representative Men, 1850

NAPOLEON BONAPARTE

By Sarah Knowles Bolton

"The series of Napoleon's successes is absolutely the most marvellous in history. No one can question that he leaves far behind the Turennes, Marlboroughs, and Fredericks; but when we bring him up for comparison an Alexander, a Hannibal, a Cæsar, a Charles, we find in the single point of marvellousness Napoleon surpassing them all . . .

"Every one of those heroes was born to a position of exceptional advantage. Two of them inherited thrones; Hannibal inherited a position royal in all but the name; Cæsar inherited an eminent position in a great empire. But Napoleon, who rose as high as any of them, began life as an obscure provincial, almost as a man without a country. It is this marvellousness which paralyzes our judgment. We seem to see at once a genius beyond all estimate, a unique character, and a fortune utterly unaccountable."

Thus wrote John Robert Seeley, Professor of Modern History in the University of Cambridge, of the man whom he regarded as the greatest enemy England has ever known.

Napoleon has been more praised and villified, probably, than any man in history. Lanfrey, though careful as to facts, and Taine, are bitter, always ready to impute sinister motives. John S. C. Abbott is adulatory; Walter Scott cannot be impartial; and Bourrienne, the discarded private secretary, Madame de Rémusat, and the Duchess d'Abrantès, must be read with allowance for prejudice. Thiers, in his twenty volumes on "The Consulate and the Empire," gives a most valuable picture of the times, friendly to the great leader; John Codman Ropes's "First Napoleon" is able; and the life by William O'Connor Morris of Oxford is generally fair and interesting.

Napoleon Bonaparte was born at Ajaccio, in the Island of Corsica, Aug. 15, 1769. This date has been disputed by some authors, who claim that Napoleon was born Jan, 7, 1768. Colonel Jung, in "Bonaparte et son Temps," thinks the dates of birth of Napoleon and his brother Joseph were exchanged by the parents, who wished, in 1778, to send Napoleon to a military school at Brienne supported by the State, and he must needs be under ten years of age.

As Corsica became subject to France in June, 1769, some persons believe that Napoleon himself changed the date of his birth from 1768 to 1769, that he might appear to the French nation as a French subject; but the date, Aug. 15, 1769, is usually accepted as correct.

The Bonaparte family were originally from the nobility of Florence, where they had taken a somewhat prominent part in politics and literature. They had lost their fortune; and Charles Bonaparte, the father of Napoleon, earned his living by the law. He was an eloquent man, and an adjutant under Pasquale Paoli, a patriot of Corsica. This island, in the fourteenth century, was under Genoa. When it gained its independence under Paoli, such rights as Genoa still possessed she sold to France. As a result, in 1769 a French army of twenty-two thousand subjugated the island, and Paoli fled to England, where he lived for twenty years.

Charles Bonaparte, at eighteen, married a girl not yet fifteen, Letizia Ramolini, descended from a noble family of Naples, a person of unusual beauty and strength of character. Although so young, she entered heartily into the warfare for Corsican independence, and shared the perils of her husband at the front.

Napoleon was the fourth of her thirteen children, the eldest, a son, and the second, a daughter, both dying young. He was born in the midst of war. He wrote Paoli, in 1789, when he was twenty years old, "I was born when my country was sinking; the cries of the dying, the groans of the oppressed, and the tears of despair surrounded my cradle from my birth."

The Duchess d'Abrantès tells this story of Napoleon's boyhood. When he was seven years old, being accused by one of his sisters of eating a basket of grapes and figs, although he denied the offence, he was whipped and kept on bread and cheese for three days.

On the fourth day a little friend of the family arrived at the home, and confessed that she and Napoleon's sister, Marianna (afterward Elisa) had eaten the fruit. The lad was asked why he had not accused his sister, and replied that he suspected that she was guilty, but said nothing out of consideration for the friend.

After the submission of Corsica to France in 1769, Count Marbœuf was appointed viceroy of the island. He became a friend of the Bonapartes; and Charles, the father, was made king's assessor to the Judicial Court for Ajaccio. Through Marbœuf's influence three of the Bonaparte children were placed in fine schools,—Joseph, Marianna, and Napoleon, the last at the military school of Brienne, near Paris. Here he remained for five years. He was a quiet, studious lad, devoted to Plutarch's Lives and Cæsar's Commentaries. He was always trying to find out what made certain men great. He was easily at the head of his class in mathematics. His industry and perseverance were astonishing.

"During play-hours," says Bourrienne, "he used to withdraw to the library, where he read works of history, particularly Polybius and Plutarch. I often went off to play with my comrades, and left him by himself in the library."

He was cold in manner, talked very little with his classmates, and felt keenly his poverty and the submission of his country to France.

Most of the boys at the school were rich, and they often ridiculed Napoleon and his country. And yet he bore them no ill-will; and, says Bourrienne, "when he had the supervision of any duty which they infringed, he would rather go to prison than denounce the criminals." During the winter of 1783-84, when the fall of snow was unusually heavy, Napoleon, then fourteen, suggested to his mates that they build a snow fort, "divide ourselves into sections, form a siege, and I will undertake to direct the attacks." This sham war was carried on with great enthusiasm for a fortnight.

Three of the best scholars were sent every year from each of the twelve provincial military schools of France to the Military College of Paris. Napoleon was one of the three sent from Brienne.

Here the young men lived so expensively that the youth of fifteen wrote a letter of protest to the Vice-Principal Berton of Brienne. He urged that, instead of so many attendants, and two-course dinners, they should wait upon themselves, clean their own boots, and eat the coarse bread made for soldiers. Temperance and activity would fit them, he said, for the hardships of war.

Napoleon won the admiration of his teachers. The professor in history, M. de l'Eguille, said: "A Corsican by birth and character, he will do something great if circumstances favor him."

After a year at this school, he was made second lieutenant of artillery in the regiment of La Fère, in 1785. The next five years he passed at different military stations in France. He was always studying. He pored over maps and plans of fortresses. He read with avidity books on law, philosophy, theology, political economy, and various forms of government. He wrote an essay on the question, "What are the institutions most likely to contribute to human happiness?" He also wrote a history of Corsica and her wrongs.

Abbott relates that on a day of public festivity at Marseilles, Napoleon was criticised because he did not join in the amusements. He replied, "It is not by playing and dancing that a *man* is to be formed."

At Auxonne, Napoleon and some other officers boarded with

a plain barber. The wife of the barber did not like the taciturn young Napoleon, who stayed in his room and devoured his books, while the other officers pleased her from their social ways, and enjoyment of the gossip of the town.

Years after, Napoleon, who had won several victories, passed that way. He asked the barber's wife if she remembered an officer by the name of Bonaparte in her home. "Indeed I do," was the reply, "and a very disagreeable inmate he was. He was always either shut up in his room, or, if he walked out, he never condescended to speak to any one."

"Ah, my good woman," said Napoleon, "had I passed my time as you wished to have me, I should not now have been in command of the army of Italy."

Napoleon was at this time very slight in physique, five feet six and a half inches tall, with a very large head, pale face, piercing eyes of grayish blue, brown hair, a smile that could be sweet and captivating, and beautiful hands.

In 1791, when he was twenty-two years old, Napoleon, now first lieutenant, visited Corsica on furlough. Remaining too long, his name was struck off the army lists. He returned to Paris, and anxiously looked about for some way to earn a living. He met his schoolmate, Bourrienne, who usually paid for any meal they took together at a restaurant, as, although poor, he was richer than Napoleon. Each day they had projects for earning money. They found some houses building, and desired to rent them, and then underlet them, but the owners asked too much to realize any profit. Napoleon solicited employment at the war office. "Everything failed," says Bourrienne.

Bonaparte's mother, left a widow with eight children in 1785, was, of course, powerless to help Napoleon. Her husband had gone on business to Montpellier in the south of France, and died of a cancerous ulcer in the stomach in the thirty-ninth year of his age. His wife was only thirty-five. Madame Bonaparte was possessed of wonderful energy, great strength of will, and excellent judgment. These her son Napoleon inherited in a marked degree.

She proved equal to the care of her fatherless children. "She managed everything," said Napoleon, "provided for everything with a prudence which could neither have been expected from her sex nor from her age. Ah, what a woman! Where shall we look for her equal? She watched over us with a solicitude unexampled. Every low sentiment, every ungenerous affection, was discouraged and discarded. She suffered nothing but that which was grand and elevated to take root in our youthful understandings. She abhorred falsehood, and would not tolerate the slightest act of disobedience. None of our faults were overlooked. Losses, privations, fatigue, had no effect upon her. She endured all, braved all. She had the energy of a man, combined with the gentleness and delicacy of a woman."

When Bonaparte was waiting in Paris for some position to open, the French Revolution had begun. On June 20, 1792, a ragged mob of five or six thousand men surrounded the Tuileries, put a red cap on the head of Louis XVI., and made him show himself at the windows to the crowd in the garden. Napoleon was indignant, and said to Bourrienne, "Why have they let in all that rabble? They should sweep off four or five hundred of them with the cannon; the rest would then set off fast enough."

Napoleon also witnessed the storming of the Tuileries on Aug. 10, when the Swiss guards were massacred. Although a Republican in sentiment, he had no sympathy with the extreme democracy of the Jacobins, and said: "If I were compelled to choose between the old monarchy and Jacobin misrule, I should infinitely prefer the former."

Years later, when Napoleon was Emperor, when asked to allow a person to return to France who had been prominent in the downfall of the Bourbon dynasty, he said, "Let him know that I am not powerful enough to protect the wretches who voted for the death of Louis XVI. from the contempt and indignation of the public."

Corsica and Paoli (who had returned and become her governor) were shocked at the excesses of the French Revolution, and hoped and planned once more for independence. Finding themselves unable to achieve it alone, they sought the aid of England. Bonaparte and his family favored adherence to France, and were banished from the island, their home plundered, and they made their escape at midnight to Marseilles. Here they were for some time in extreme poverty. Joseph, the eldest son, found employment as a clerk in an office, and in August, 1794, married Julia Clari, the daughter of one of the richest merchants of Marseilles. This was a great pecuniary benefit to the whole family.

Napoleon had finally been reinstated in the army; for with the Reign of Terror at home, and wars with monarchies abroad, all fearful of the growth of republican sentiments and consequent revolutions, the French army was in need of all its able young men.

Napoleon's first important work was at the siege of Toulon. This was the great naval depot and arsenal of France. The Royalists, or followers of the Bourbon king, Louis XVI., had centred here, and, opposed to the republic, had surrendered the city, with its forts and ships, to England.

The place must be retaken; and the Republic sent out an army under Carteaux, a portrait painter. For some months the siege was carried on, but almost nothing was accomplished. Sixty thousand men were needed, and Carteaux had but twenty-five thousand.

Napoleon, on his way from Avignon to Nice, passed through Toulon, stopping to see a friend who introduced him to Carteaux. The young officer saw at once the mistakes of the campaign. "Instead of attacking the town," said Napoleon, "try and establish batteries which shall sweep the harbor and the roadstead. If you can only drive away the ships, the troops will not remain."

Cape l'Eguillette separates the two harbors, and here batteries were placed to sweep the sea; for Napoleon had said, putting his finger on the map, at the cape, "Toulon is there!"

As he predicted, the English ships were driven off after a terrible bombardment; fifteen thousand of the inhabitants of Toulon in dismay fled to the ships of the allies; the plan of Napoleon had proved a great success.

He was not responsible for the horrors which followed. The Royalists set fire to the arsenal and ships before their departure; while the town was in flames, cannon from the shore sunk boat-loads of fugitives, and hundreds in the city who could not escape were deliberately shot in the streets and in their homes, so desperate had become the hate between Royalists and Republicans, or really Jacobins.

Fouché, afterwards prominent under the Empire, wrote to a friend, Dec. 23: "We have only one way of celebrating victory. This evening we shoot two hundred and thirteen rebels. Adieu, my friend; tears of joy run down my cheeks, and my heart is overflowing."

"It was," says Walter Scott, concerning this taking of Toulon, Dec. 17, 1793, "upon this night of terror, conflagration, tears, and blood, that the star of Napoleon first ascended the horizon; and, though it gleamed over many a scene of horror ere it set, it may be doubted whether its light was ever blended with that of one more dreadful."

For this brilliant undertaking Napoleon was made General of Artillery. General Dugommier, who commanded at Toulon, said, "Promote this young officer, or he will promote himself." Napoleon was wounded in his thigh by a bayonet thrust in one of the charges. He was at this time but twenty-four years of age, poor, ambitious, and with little prospect of his future wonderful career.

He was sent to defend the coast of Provence, and was denounced by the Jacobins, who said he was building a bastile at Marseilles to enslave the people. In March, 1794, he rejoined the army of Italy at Nice, and was so useful that the commander-in-chief wrote: "I am indebted to the comprehensive talents of General Bonaparte for the plans which have insured our victory."

In July, 1794, he was sent on a mission to Genoa, to examine the fortresses and the neighboring country. Meantime, one set of French leaders had been superseded by a set equally bad. Through jealousy, and as a friend of the younger Robespierre, Napoleon was arrested as a "suspected person," was two weeks in prison, and nearly lost his life. He seems to have been spared for the selfish reason, "the possible utility of the military and local knowledge of the said Bonaparte." He addressed an eloquent letter to his accusers, quoted by Lanfrey, in which he says: "Remove the oppression which surrounds me; give me back the esteem of patriots. An hour afterwards, if bad men wish for my life, I care so little for it, I have so often counted it for nothing . . . Yes, nothing but the idea that it may be of use to the country gives me courage to bear its weight."

Soon after this, to scatter such officers as himself, who were supposed to be Jacobin in tendency, Napoleon was ordered to La Vendée to put down civil dissensions. He rebelled against being separated from the army of Italy. "You are too young," said Aubrey, the Girondist deputy, "to be commander-in-chief of artillery."

"Men age fast on a field of battle," said Napoleon, "and I am no exception."

For refusing to proceed to his post, Napoleon's name was struck off the army lists, and again he was in Paris, out of employment. When he and Bourrienne took a stroll at evening on the Boulevards, and saw the rich young men on horseback, apparently living a life of ease and luxury, "dandies with their whiskers," says Madame Junot (Duchess d'Abrantès), Napoleon would exclaim bitterly, "And it is on such beings as these that Fortune confers her favors. How contemptible is human nature!"

He told Count Montholon, when in exile at St. Helena, that at this time he came near committing suicide by throwing himself into the river. With head down, and meditating upon his determination, he ran against a plainly dressed man, who proved to be Démasis, a former comrade in the artillery. "What is the matter?" he said to Napoleon. "You do not listen to me! You do not seem glad to see me! What misfortune threatens you? You look to me like a madman about to kill himself." Napoleon told him his needs, and his mother's poverty. "Is that all?" said Démasis. "Here are six thousand dollars in gold, which I can spare without any inconvenience. Take them, and relieve your mother."

Hardly aware of what he was doing, Napoleon grasped the money, and sent it to his mother. Afterwards he could find nothing of Démasis. Fifteen years later, when the Empire was near its fall, Napoleon met him, made him accept sixty thousand dollars to repay the loan of six thousand, and appointed him director-general of the crown gardens, at a salary of six thousand dollars a year, and the honors of an officer in the household. He also provided a good situation for Démasis' brother.

He never forgot a kindness. A humble shoemaker, who worked for him in these days of poverty, and waited for his pay, was always employed by Napoleon after he became Emperor, though he was urged to go to some one more fashionable. A jeweller, who once trusted him, was remembered in Napoleon's days of prosperity, and thus made his fortune. To a lady, a stranger to him, who once was kind to him in sickness in these early years, he sent two thousand dollars, hearing that her circumstances had changed. To an old man in Jersey, who had once loaned his father twenty-five louis, he sent ten times that sum.

Reverses began to attend the army of Italy. Whenever it was convenient to use his services, it seemed always to be remembered that he had knowledge and sagacity. Napoleon was asked by the director of military affairs to draw up a plan of operations for the army. It was sent to Kellermann, commander-in-chief of the army of Italy, who rejected it, saving, "The author is a fit inmate for a lunatic asylum." Lanfrey and other historians consider the plan altogether brilliant and admirable.

Napoleon, by years of study, had made himself a master in the science of war, as well as along other lines. He had made himself ready for a great opportunity, and a great opportunity came to him.

France, in her struggle for self-government, had adopted a new constitution, under a Directory of five persons, with a Council of two hundred and fifty Ancients, and a Council of Five Hundred, somewhat like our House of Representatives. The new government, though acceptable to the provinces, did not please either the Royalists or Jacobins of Paris, and the people, now so used to bloodshed, resorted to force to destroy the Directory.

Barras, one of the Directors, who knew Napoleon, immediately thought of him as a young man who could quell a mob. "It is that little Corsican officer," he said, "who will not stand upon ceremony!" The Directory had but about eight thousand soldiers; the National Guard numbered forty thousand. Napoleon spent the whole night in turning the Louvre and the Tuileries into a sort of camp, with artillery posted at all the outlets. He armed all the members of the government, that they might defend themselves if the necessity arose, and he took care to leave a way of retreat open to St. Cloud.

The National Guards appeared on the morning of Oct. 5, 1795 (13th Vendémiaire, as the month was called by the Revolutionary Calendar), in front of Napoleon's troops. All day the two armies were within fifteen paces of each other. At four o'clock in the afternoon, General Danican of the National Guards gave the signal for attack. Napoleon mounted his horse, and the fight began at several places.

The cannon swept them down at every point. At six o'clock the battle was over, and order was restored in Paris. About eighty only were killed, and three or four hundred wounded, as the guns were loaded with powder after two discharges. Napoleon was, as he deserved to be, the hero of the hour. With the utmost self-possession, with a clear brain and never-failing courage, he had been equal to the emergency.

Napoleon was made General of the Interior, with the command of Paris. The days of poverty were over. He found places for several of his family, and was much sought after by those in high position. He was especially good to the poor, and the Duchess d'Abrantès tells how he climbed to attics and went down into cellars to feed the hungry. As he was stepping out of his carriage one day at the home of the Duchess, a woman held her dead child before him. It had died from want. She had come to ask him to save her other children. "If nobody will give me anything," she said, "I must even take them all five and drown myself with them." Napoleon remembered how near he had been to drowning himself only a little time before. He obtained the wages due to her husband, who had been killed while at work on the roof of the Tuileries, and a pension was granted her.

Soon after this an attractive boy about fourteen years of age came to Napoleon and asked for the sword of his father, who was a general of the Republic, and had been put to death by the Jacobins, because he was a Girondist, or moderate Republican.

"I was so touched by this affectionate request," said Napoleon, "that I ordered it to be given to him. This boy was Eugène Beauharnais. On seeing the sword he burst into tears. I felt so affected by his conduct, that I noticed and praised him much. A few days afterwards his mother came to return me a visit of thanks. I was struck with her appearance, and still more with her *esprit*."

The young general of twenty-six became thoroughly in love with the graceful and lovable widow of thirty-two. Josephine Tascher, the only child of French parents, had been born in the Island of Martinique, Jan. 24, 1763. She was married when sixteen to Viscount de Beauharnais, a major in the army, who introduced her to the court of Marie Antoinette, but who, with all his wealth and position, did not make her life a happy one. After four years of marriage and the birth of two children, Hortense and Eugène, to whom she was most tenderly attached, she and Beauharnais separated, and she returned to Martinique, but at his persistent request she came back to him after three years.

On his imprisonment during the Reign of Terror she attempted to save him and was thrown into prison, where she narrowly escaped the guillotine. He was beheaded July 23, 1794.

"Josephine," says Meneval, the secretary of Napoleon after Bourrienne, "was irresistibly attractive . . . Her temper was always the same. She was gentle and kind, affable and indulgent with every one, without difference of persons. She had neither a superior mind nor much learning; but her exquisite politeness, her full acquaintance with society, with the court, and with their innocent artifices, made her always know the best things to say or do."

Napoleon found at the home of Madame de Beauharnais the most noted persons in Paris, and, what was more important for his happiness, the one woman whom he ever after loved.

Years later he said, "Josephine was truly a most lovely woman, refined, affable, and charming . . . She was so kind, so humane— she was the most graceful lady and the best woman in France. I never saw her act inelegantly during the whole time we lived together. She possessed a perfect knowledge of the different shades of my character, and evinced the most exquisite tact in turning this knowledge to the best account . . .

"I was the object of her deepest attachment. If I went into my carriage at midnight for a long journey, there, to my surprise, I found her, seated before me and awaiting my arrival. If I attempted to dissuade her from accompanying me, she had so many good and affectionate reasons to urge, that it was almost always necessary to yield. In a word, she always proved to me a happy and affectionate wife, and I have preserved the tenderest recollections of her."

Barras, the ardent friend of Josephine, urged her marriage with Napoleon, and her children favored it. She admired him, but hesitated. She wrote a friend, "Barras assures me that if I marry the general, he will obtain for him the appointment of commander-in-chief of the army of Italy. Yesterday Bonaparte, speaking to me of this favor, which has already caused some jealousy among his companions in arms, although it is not yet granted, said, 'Do they think I need patronage to insure my success? Some day they will be only too happy if I grant them mine. My sword is at my side, and that will carry me a long way.'"

They were married March 9, 1796, Napoleon having been appointed to the command of the army of Italy on the preceding 23d of February. He remained in Paris but a few days, and then hastened to his army, reaching Nice towards the last of March.

He found an army of about thirty thousand men, "without pay, without provisions, without shoes," opposed to about twice their number of Austrians and Sardinians. He issued an address to them: "Soldiers, you are poorly fed and half-naked. The government owes you much, but can do nothing for you. Your patience, your courage, do you honor, but they bring you no advantage, no glory. I am about to lead you into the most fertile plains in the world; there you will find larger cities and rich provinces; there you will find honor, glory, and wealth. Soldiers of Italy, shall you lack courage?"

His soldiers, who till his death idolized him and would die for him, were soon to prove on scores of battle-fields that they never lacked courage.

This slight, boyish-looking general of twenty-six said to his veteran officers, "We must hurl ourselves on the foe like a thunderbolt, and smite like it."

And this was done. The first battle was on April 12, at Montenotte. The Austrians were routed, leaving their colors and cannon with the French, and three thousand dead and wounded. Napoleon afterwards said to the Emperor of Austria, "My title of nobility dates from the battle of Montenotte."

The battles of Millesimo and Mondovi quickly followed. On the heights of Monte Zemolo, Napoleon looked out upon the fertile plains of Italy, and exclaimed, "Hannibal crossed the

Alps, but we have turned them!"

Then he addressed his enthusiastic soldiers: "In fifteen days," he said, "you have won six victories; captured twenty-one flags, fifty cannon, many fortified places; conquered the richest part of Piedmont; you have captured fifteen thousand prisoners, and killed and wounded ten thousand men. You lacked everything; you have gained battles without cannon; crossed rivers without bridges; made forced marches without shoes; often bivouacked without bread; the Republican phalanxes were alone capable of such extraordinary deeds. Soldiers, receive your due of thanks!"

Murat, his aide-de-camp, who afterwards married Napoleon's sister Caroline, and became King of Naples, was sent to Paris with the armistice proposed by the King of Sardinia, and Junot with the flags, which caused the greatest rejoicing. *Fêtes* were celebrated at the Champ de Mars, and Napoleon's name was honored as the conqueror of Italy.

Napoleon writes to his bride: "Your letters are the delight of my days, and my happy days are not very many. Junot is carrying twenty-two flags to Paris. You must come back with him; do you understand? It would be hopeless misery, an inconsolable grief, continual agony, if I should have the misfortune of seeing him come back alone, my adorable one . . . You will be here, by my side, on my heart, in my arms! Take wings, come, come! But travel slowly; the way is long, bad, and tiresome."

Almost daily he writes to his wife: "My only Josephine, away from you, there is no happiness; away from you, the world is a desert, in which I stand alone, with no chance of tasting the delicious joy of pouring out my heart. You have robbed me of more than my soul; you are the sole thought of my life. If I am worn out by all the torment of events, and fear the issue; if men disgust me; if I am ready to curse life, I place my hand on my heart,—your image is beating there."

She is not well, and does not come to him, and again he writes: "My dear, do remember to tell me that you are certain that I love you more than can be imagined; ... that no hour passes that I do not think of you; that it has never entered my mind to think of any other woman; ... that you, as I see you, as you are, can please me and absorb my whole soul; that you have wholly filled it; that my heart has no corner that you do not see, no thoughts that are not subordinate to you; that my strength, my arms, my intelligence, are all yours; ... and that the day when you shall have changed, or shall have ceased to live, will be the day of my death; that nature, the earth, is beautiful, in my eyes, only because you live on it."

General Marmont says in his memoirs: "Bonaparte, however occupied he may have been with his greatness, the interests intrusted to him, and with his future, had, nevertheless, time to devote to feelings of another sort; he was continually thinking of his wife . . . He often spoke to me of her, and of his love, with all the frankness, fire, and illusion of a very young man . . . During a trip we made together at this time, to inspect the places in Piedmont that had fallen into our hands, one morning, at Tortona, the glass in front of his wife's portrait, which he always carried with him, broke in his hands. He grew frightfully pale, and suffered the keenest alarm."

Again he says, "Never did a purer, truer, or more exclusive love fill a man's heart, or the heart of so extraordinary a man."

Lanfrey says, "In this love, which has been said to be the only one that touched his heart, all the fire and flame of his masterful nature showed itself."

Napoleon pushed on his troops to conquer the Austrian Beaulieu, crossed the river Po at Piacenza, and overtook the enemy at the town of Lodi on the Adda River. The town was taken by the French; nut, to cross the Adda and reach Beaulieu, it was necessary to storm a narrow wooden bridge, which was defended by artillery and by from twelve to sixteen thousand Austrians. Napoleon immediately placed a battery on his own side of the river, sent a detachment of cavalry to ford the river and attack the enemy's rear, and then, at the head of several thousand men, bade them force a passage across the bridge.

The French were mowed down by the Austrian cannon. They wavered, when Napoleon seized a standard, and, with Lannes and one or two other officers, rushed among the troops and inspired them to gain a complete victory. Lannes was the first to cross the bridge and reach the Austrian gunners, who were sabred at their guns, and Napoleon the second. Lannes was promoted on the spot for his valor. So proud were the troops that their general should fight in the ranks, that they ever after called him their "Little Corporal." The conflict was a bloody one. The Austrian loss was much heavier than the French.

Napoleon said, "It was not till after the *terrible passage of the bridge of Lodi* that the idea shot across my mind that I might become a decisive actor in the political arena. Then arose, for the first time, the spark of great ambition."

He said to his aide-de-camp, Marmont, "In our time, no one has devised anything great; I must set an example."

On May 15, 1796, Napoleon entered Milan in triumph. The people hated the rule of Austria, and hoped for liberty under the French Republic. A triumphal arch was erected in the city, and flowers were scattered in the path of the French. To his soldiers, "who had rushed," he said, "like a torrent from the height of the Apennines," Napoleon gave all the glory.

In accordance with the wishes of the Directory in France, he levied twenty million francs on Milan, and took some of her best art works to Paris. The army was supported by the countries through which it passed, as was Sherman's in our Civil War.

Late in June, Josephine reached Milan, and for a brief period they were happy; but Napoleon was obliged very soon to be at the front. The war now centred about Mantua, which was strongly fortified. Seven or eight thousand French troops were besieging it, when it was ascertained that Würmser, the Austrian general, was marching against the French with seventy thousand men, in three armies, while Napoleon had but about forty-five thousand.

At once the siege of Mantua was raised, the gun-carriages burned, the powder thrown into the river, the cannon spiked, and the French forces were led against Würmser.

Napoleon, with his usual celerity and tact,—he used to say, "War, like government, is mainly decided by tact,"—managed to defeat each of the three Austrian armies in turn.

At Lonato the Austrians lost ten thousand in killed, wounded, and prisoners. The day after the battle, one of the Austrian divisions, reduced to four thousand men, wandered into Lonato, and demanded the surrender of the garrison of twelve hundred. Napoleon called his staff together; and when the bandage was removed from the eyes of the officer, he said with authority, "Go and tell your general that I give him eight minutes to lay down his arms!" The Austrians surrendered, and were soon chagrined to find that four thousand had succumbed to twelve hundred Frenchmen.

Napoleon said at Lonato, "I was at ease; the Thirty-second was there!" So rejoiced were the men at these words that they had them embroidered on their regimental flag.

In this short campaign twenty thousand Austrians had been killed and wounded, fifteen thousand taken prisoners, with seventy pieces of artillery, and twenty-two stands of colors. The latter were sent to Paris.

Early in September, Napoleon again defeated Würmser at Bassano. After the battle, at midnight Napoleon rode over the battle-field by moonlight, the quiet broken only by the moans of the wounded and dying. Suddenly a dog sprang from beneath the cloak of his dead master, rushed to Napoleon as though asking aid, and then back to the body, licking the face and hands of the dead, and howling piteously.

Napoleon was strongly moved, and said years afterward, "I know not how it was, but no incident upon any field of battle ever produced so deep an impression upon my feelings. 'This man,' thought I, 'must have had among his comrades friends, and yet here he lies forsaken by all except his faithful dog.' ... Certainly, in that moment, I should have been unable to refuse any request to a suppliant enemy."

When at St. Helena, Madame Montholon, seeming to be afraid of a dog, Napoleon said, "He who does not love a dog has never known what real fidelity means."

Austria soon put another general in the field with over sixty thousand men. She was determined not to lose Italy. At first the French army lost some battles, the general-in-chief not being with them. When he came to his army, he said to some regiments, "Soldiers, I am not satisfied with you. You have shown neither discipline, constancy, nor courage . . . Let it be written on the colors, 'They are not of the army of Italy.'"

The men seemed heart-broken. "Place us in the van of the army," they said, "and you shall then judge whether we do not belong to the army of Italy."

They were soon put to the test. Napoleon marched out of Verona on the night of Nov. 14, descended the Adige river, and fell upon the rear of Alvinzi, the Austrian general, at Arcola. The village is surrounded by marshes, crossed by causeways or bridges.

When the French rushed upon the bridges, they were repulsed by the guns of the Austrians. Napoleon sprang from his horse, seized a standard, and shouted, "Follow your general!" but he was borne by the struggling soldiers off the bridge into the marsh.

Frenzied at the probable loss of their general, the French fought desperately. Muiron, who had saved Napoleon at Toulon when he was wounded in the thigh, covered his general with his own body, and received his death wound from a shell. Lannes received three wounds in endeavoring to protect Napoleon, who was finally extricated, and was again at the head of the column. After three days of battle, the French were victorious. It is estimated that twenty thousand men perished in the swamps of Arcola.

Napoleon wrote a letter of sympathy to the young widow of Muiron, who in a few weeks died at the birth of a lifeless child.

To the Directory he wrote: "Never was a field of battle more valiantly disputed than the conflict at Arcola. I have scarcely any generals left. Their bravery and their patriotic enthusiasm are without example."

In the midst of this toil and carnage, Napoleon could find time to write to Josephine. She had followed him for a while after coming to Milan, but her dangers were so great that it was soon found to be impossible.

After Arcola he writes her: "At length, my adored Josephine, I live again. Death is no longer before me, and glory and honor are still in my breast . . . Soon Mantua will be ours, and then thy husband will fold thee in his arms, and give thee a thousand proofs of his ardent affection. I shall proceed to Milan as soon as I can; I am a little fatigued. I have received letters from Eugène and Hortense. I am delighted with the children . . . Adieu, my adorable Josephine. Think of me often. Death alone can break the union which sympathy, love, and sentiment have formed. Let me have news of your health. A thousand and a thousand kisses."

If she does not write often he is distressed; "Three days without a word from you," he writes, "and I have written you several times. This absence is horrible; the nights are long, tiresome, dull; the days are monotonous . . . I don't really live away from you; my life's happiness is only to be with my sweet Josephine. Think of me! write to me often, very often; it is the only balm in absence which is cruel, but I hope will be short . . . Day before yesterday I was in the field all day. Yesterday I stayed in bed. A fever and a raging headache prevented me from writing to my dear one; but I received her letters. I pressed them to my heart and my lips; and the pang of absence, a hundred miles apart, vanished."

Yet, with all this intensity of feeling, Napoleon had wonderful self-command. He said, "Nature seems to have calculated that I should endure great reverses. She has given me a mind of marble. Thunder cannot ruffle it. The shaft merely glides along."

Austria made another desperate effort to overcome Napoleon

and save Würmser, shut up in Mantua. At four o'clock in the morning, Jan. 14, 1797, the battle of Rivoli began. For twelve hours Napoleon was in the hottest of the fight. Three horses were shot under him.

After a desperate but victorious battle, the troops marched all night, conquered Provera before Mantua the next day, and La Favorita on the third day. The Austrian army had lost thirty thousand men in three days, of whom twenty thousand were taken prisoners. Napoleon, in his report of the battle of Favorita, spoke of the terrible Fifty-seventh. Thereafter the Fifty-seventh adopted the name of "The Terrible," proud of this distinction of their chief.

Massena's men had marched and fought incessantly for four days and nights. No wonder the Austrians said, "The French do not march, they fly." Napoleon wrote, "The Roman legions used to make twenty-four miles a day; our men make thirty, and fight in the intervals." ...

Würmser surrendered Mantua Feb. 3, 1797. Twenty-seven thousand men had died of wounds or sickness since the commencement of the siege. The horses had all been eaten, and the city could sustain itself no longer. Würmser had declared that he could hold out for a year. But Napoleon knew that so brave a marshal as Würmser would not surrender unless reduced to the last extremity.

He therefore allowed Würmser to retire with all his staff and two thousand cavalry. He surrendered to France eighteen thousand prisoners. Würmser wished to salute the young conqueror of twenty-seven; but Napoleon had gone to Bologna, not liking to subject the marshal of seventy to humiliation. Lanfrey thinks this was done for effect, but there seems no good reason for always imputing bad motives to Napoleon. A man so worshipped by his soldiers, and, indeed, by the nation, had much that was noble and refined in his nature.

Würmser, out of gratitude to Napoleon, saved his life at Bologna, by making known to him a plot to poison him.

Napoleon now turned his attention towards the Papal States. The Pope had no love for the "godless Republic." Thousands of priests had fled from France to Rome. Austria and Rome were closely allied, and both ready to sustain war against France whenever an opportunity offered.

The Directory had written to Napoleon "that the Roman Catholic religion would always be the irreconcilable enemy of the Republic," but Napoleon bore no ill-will towards his mother's faith and the faith in which he himself died.

He issued a proclamation in which he said, "The French soldier carries in one hand the bayonet, the guaranty of victory, and in the other an olive branch, the symbol of peace and pledge of his protection."

When within three days' march of Rome, the Pope sued for peace, and the treaty of Tolentino was signed Feb. 19, 1797.

Napoleon writes to Josephine on the same day: "Peace has just been signed with Rome. Bologna, Ferrara, the Romagna, are ceded to the Republic. The Pope gives us shortly thirty million [francs] and many works of art . . .

"My dear, I beg of you think of me often, and write me every day . . . You, to whom nature has given intelligence, gentleness, and beauty, you, who rule alone over my heart, you, who doubtless know only too well the absolute power you exercise over my heart, write to me, think of me, and love me. Ever yours."

Austria was not yet humbled. Napoleon determined to march against Vienna. The young Archduke Charles, brother of the ruler of Austria, was in command of the Austrian army. "He is a man," said Napoleon, "whose conduct can never attract blame . . . More than all, he is a good man, and that includes everything when said of a prince."

Charles had beaten Napoleon's generals on the Rhine, but he could not beat the "Little Corporal." His fifty thousand men melted away as they fled, wounded and distracted, over the Alps.

When within sight of Vienna, Napoleon proposed peace; and

Austria, tired of war for a time at least, accepted the conditions. Early in May, France declared war against the Venetian Republic. The latter had been neutral, although both Austrians and French had crossed her territory. Her aristocracy had no sympathy with the French Republic, and preferred Austria. Perhaps to guard herself from both nations, she raised an army of sixty thousand men, and put herself in the attitude of armed neutrality. She refused to ally herself to France. "Be neutral, then," said Napoleon; "but remember, if you violate your neutrality, if you harass my troops, if you cut off my supplies, I will take ample vengeance . . . The hour that witnesses the treachery of Venice shall terminate her independence."

Whether or not her government desired to keep the peace, insurrections arose among the people in Verona and elsewhere, French soldiers were killed, Napoleon took "ample vengeance," and in the treaty of Campo Formio, Oct. 17, 1797, Venice was handed over to Austria. The Republic ceased to exist. In taking the hated oath of allegiance to Austria, the ex-Doge of Venice became insensible, and died soon after.

Napoleon now returned to Milan, and for a time lived in peace and happiness at the Serbelloni Palace. Josephine won every heart by her grace and her kindness. Napoleon said, "I conquer provinces, but Josephine wins hearts."

Madame de Rémusat wrote: "Love seemed to come every day to place at her feet a new conquest over a people entranced with its conqueror."

The people waited to see Napoleon pass in and out of his palace. They did him honor as though he were a king. He had sent for his mother, his brothers Joseph and Louis, and his beautiful sister Pauline, sixteen years of age, of whom Arnault, the poet, said, "if she was the prettiest person in the world, she was also the most frivolous."

Imbert de Saint-Amand, in his "Citizeness Bonaparte," quotes this incident to show Josephine's power over her husband. "He was absolutely faithful to her," says Saint-Amand, "and this at a time when there was not a beauty in Milan who was not setting her cap for him."

Josephine owned a pug dog, Fortuné, which, when she was imprisoned in the Reign of Terror, was brought to her cell with a letter concealed in his collar. Ever since she had been extremely fond of him. They were all at the Castle of Montebello, a few leagues from Milan, during the warm weather. "You see that fellow there?" said Napoleon to Arnault, pointing to the dog who lay on the sofa beside his mistress, "he is my rival. When I married I wanted to put him out of my wife's room, but I was given to understand that I might go away myself or share it with him. I was annoyed; but it was to take or to leave, and I yielded. The favorite was not so accommodating, and he left his mark on my leg."

Fortuné barked at everything, and used to bite other dogs. The cook's dog, a mastiff, returned the bite one day, and killed Fortuné. Josephine was in despair; but the mischief was done, and there was no help for it.

Nov. 17 Napoleon left Milan, and, after a continued ovation along the route, reached Paris Dec. 5, where, a change having taken place in the government, he thought it wise to be for a time. Though the Directory was jealous of the rising power of Napoleon, the people demanded a magnificent reception for him, which was prepared in the Luxembourg.

Napoleon made an address which was eagerly listened to, and the people were wild with enthusiasm. Thiers says, "All heads were overcome with the intoxication." Talleyrand gave a great ball costing over twelve thousand francs. Bourrienne, his secretary, remarked that it must be agreeable to "see his fellow-citizens so eagerly running after him."

"Bah! the people would crowd as fast to see me if I were going to the scaffold," was Napoleon's reply. So well did he understand human nature.

He said to Bourrienne, "Were I to remain in Paris long, doing nothing, I should be lost. In this great Babylon one reputation displaces another. Let me be seen but three times at the theatre and I shall no longer excite attention; so I shall go there but seldom."

Napoleon was made a member of the Institute, in the class of the Sciences and Arts. This honor he greatly valued, writing to the president of the class, "I feel well assured that, before I can be their equal, I must long be their scholar . . . True conquests—the only ones which leave no regret behind them—are those which are made over ignorance. The most honorable, as well as the most useful, occupation for nations is the contributing to the extension of human knowledge."

"He had," says Bourrienne, "an extreme aversion to mediocrity," or to people who are too indolent to read and improve themselves. "Mankind," he said, "are, in the end, always governed by superiority of intellectual qualities."

The Directory were anxious for an attack upon England, which had joined the Coalition against France in 1793, and was her most formidable enemy. "Go there," said Barras, "and capture the giant Corsair that infests the seas; go punish in London outrages that have too long gone unpunished."

Arnault said to Napoleon, "The Directory wishes to get you away; France wishes to keep you."

"I am perfectly willing to make a tour of the coast," said Napoleon to Bourrienne. "Should the expedition to Britain prove too hazardous, as I much fear that it will, the army of England will become the army of the East, and we will go to Egypt." He spent a week in looking over the ground, and said, "I will not hazard it. I would not thus sport with the fate of France."

He determined to colonize Egypt. He would take with him men of science, artists, and artisans. He said to Montholon at St. Helena, "Were the French once established in Egypt, it would be impossible for the English to maintain themselves long in India. Squadrons constructed on the shores of the Red Sea, provisioned with the products of the country, and equipped and manned by the French troops stationed in Egypt, would infallibly make us masters of India, and at a moment when England least expected it."

The fleet set sail from Toulon May 19, 1798, with forty thousand men besides ten thousand sailors. Josephine came to Toulon to say good-by, and wished to go with her husband, but this would have been most unwise.

The fleet arrived off Malta June 10, which, with almost no opposition, surrendered to the French its twelve hundred pieces of cannon, its ten thousand pounds of powder, its ships, and its forty thousand muskets.

On June 30 the fleet appeared before Alexandria, which was soon captured. Then the army set out to cross the desert towards Cairo.

The heat was intense, they suffered for lack of water, and murmured at the Directory. Napoleon bivouacked in their midst, and dined on lentils.

On July 21 they came in sight of the Pyramids. The whole army halted. "Soldiers," said Napoleon, "from the summit of those pyramids forty centuries look down upon you!"

Before them lay the intrenched camp of Embabeh, with ten thousand Mameluke horsemen under Mourad Bey. These charged upon the immovable squares of the French only to be cut to pieces by bayonets.

They fought desperately, but were routed, and many of them driven into the Nile. Over two thousand perished, while the French did not lose over one hundred and fifty in killed and wounded. "The banks of the Nile," says Bourrienne, "were strewed with heaps of bodies, which the waves were every moment washing into the sea." The soldiers bent their bayonets into hooks, and for days fished up the bodies of the Mamelukes, on each of which they found from five to six hundred louis in gold.

Ten days after this battle of the Pyramids, the French fleet was destroyed by Nelson in the terrible battle of the Nile. Admiral Brueys was killed, and the bodies of his men seemed to fill the Bay of Aboukir.

Napoleon was virtually a prisoner in Egypt. The blow was irreparable. The army was despondent, but Napoleon was calm. "Unfortunate Brueys," he said, "what have you done!"

It was evident that he must organize Egypt as soon as possible. He established in Cairo an Institute of Arts and Sciences, he built factories, and he planned two canals, one uniting the Red Sea with the Mediterranean across the Isthmus of Suez, and the other connecting the Red Sea with the Nile at Cairo.

Meantime France was threatened with war on every side. Russia and Turkey had joined hands with England and Austria. They were sweeping over Italy. Turkey had raised an army in Syria, and Napoleon hastened thither with thirteen thousand men over a desert of seventy-five leagues.

He took El Arish Feb. 20, 1799, then Gaza; then Jaffa was taken by assault, as the garrison refused to yield, and beheaded the messenger sent to them, putting his head on a pole. The massacre which followed was horrible. Some two thousand prisoners were taken to the seashore and shot by Napoleon's order. Bourrienne says, Napoleon "yielded only in the last extremity, and was one of those, perhaps, who beheld the massacre with the deepest pain."

Napoleon has been greatly blamed for this act. These men would, of course, have gone back to the enemy, and the Turks themselves give no quarter; and yet, for humanity's sake, one wishes that they could have been spared.

After the battle at Jaffa the French began the siege of St. Jean d'Acre, where Djezzar, which name signifies butcher, the head of the army, resided. The siege lasted sixty days. Sir Sidney Smith of England, with two ships of war, assisted the fort, and Phélippeaux, an old schoolmate of Napoleon at Brienne, directed the artillery. Napoleon's battering train, sent forward by sea, had been taken by the English. The siege had to be raised, four thousand of the French being disabled, and the army retreated to Jaffa. The plague was decimating the ranks;

and Napoleon, to inspire his men, went among the plague-stricken soldiers and often touched them. The wounded and sick were carried on horses, while Napoleon and all his officers went on foot. Napoleon said, "Sir Sidney Smith made me miss my destiny."

Napoleon defeated the Turks at Aboukir, July 25, with a loss to them of ten thousand men, and then, learning of the perilous condition of France in her wars with the allied powers, hastened to Paris, leaving General Kléber in charge in Egypt. Napoleon narrowly missed being captured by the English cruisers.

France was overjoyed at his return. Bells were rung and bonfires kindled. He reached Paris Oct. 16, 1799. Josephine had gone to Lyons to meet him. He had started for Paris by a different route, and she missed him.

When she returned Napoleon refused to see her. While in Egypt Junot had foolishly told him some gossip about Josephine, who was obliged to be courteous to everybody, which had made him jealous. It probably came from Napoleon's brothers, who disliked her great influence over him.

Josephine was nearly heart-broken. She had not seen Napoleon for a year and a half. Both Eugène and Hortense begged that Napoleon would take their mother back into his heart.

Finally he opened his door, and with a stern look at Josephine, said to Eugène, then eighteen, who had just returned with him from Egypt, "As for you, you shall not suffer for your mother's misdeeds; I shall keep you with me."

With commendable spirit, the boy, who idolized his mother, replied, "No, General; I bid you farewell on the spot."

Seeing his mistake, he pressed Eugène to his heart, folded Josephine in his arms, and sent for his brother Lucien, to show him how thoroughly he and Josephine were reconciled to each other.

Napoleon had reached Paris at an opportune moment. The Directory were disliked, and he had made up his mind to overturn the government. A dinner was given to Napoleon at the Temple of Victory by five or six hundred members of the two Councils, the Ancients, and the Five Hundred. In the evening Josephine did the honors of the drawing-room at their own house. "She fascinated every one who came near her," says Saint-Amand, "by her exquisite grace and charming courtesy. All the brusqueness and violence of Bonaparte's manners were tempered by the soothing and insinuating gentleness of his amiable and kindly wife."

Only a few persons were in Napoleon's secret. By a provision of the Constitution, the Council of the Ancients, in case of peril to the Republic, could convoke the Legislative Body (the two Councils) outside the capital to avoid the influence of the multitude, and choose a general to command the troops to defend the legislature.

The 18th Brumaire (Nov. 9) was the day set for this Council at the Tuileries to vote to change the place of meeting to St. Cloud. It was given out that he was to take a journey, so his officers and some cavalry were to be at his house at six o'clock in the morning to go with him to the Tuileries, that he might review the troops, to be gathered there at seven.

At six o'clock, Lefebvre, the commander of the military division, had arrived. Napoleon said to him, "Here is the Turkish sabre which I carried at the battle of the Pyramids. Do you, who are one of the most valiant defenders of the country, accept it? Will you let our country perish in the hands of the pettifoggers who are ruining it?" It was gladly accepted.

All rode to the Tuileries. The Ancients voted to meet at St. Cloud on the morrow, and gave Napoleon the command of the troops.

On the 19th Brumaire the way to St. Cloud was crowded with troops and carriages. All was excitement and confusion. Napoleon's friends said, "You are marching to the guillotine." "We shall see," was his cool reply. When Napoleon arrived at St. Cloud he entered the hall of the Council of the Ancients and made a brief address. Then he went to the Council of the Five

Hundred. It was five in the afternoon. At the sight of him they shouted, "Down with the Dictator! Down with the tyrant!" They brandished daggers and threatened his life. His soldiers hastened to his aid; and one grenadier, Thomé, had his clothes cut by a dagger. Bourrienne says they were simply torn. Lucien Bonaparte, the president of the Five Hundred, left his seat in disgust at the tumult. He called upon the general and the soldiers "to execute the vote of the Ancients." The drums were beaten, the soldiers entered the hall, the deputies fled in every direction, and the old government was a thing of the past. Three consuls were elected, of whom Napoleon was the First Consul. He rode home at three in the morning. At thirty he had conquered France as well as Italy.

There is no doubt that a large majority of the people of France were rejoiced at the change in government. "Napoleon," says Alison in his History of Europe, "rivalled Cæsar in the clemency with which he used his victory. No proscriptions or massacres, few arrests or imprisonments, followed the triumph of order over revolution. On the contrary, numerous acts of mercy, as wise as they were magnanimous, illustrated the rise of the consular throne. The elevation of Napoleon was not only unstained by blood, but not even a single captive long lamented the ear of the victor."

On the 19th of February, 1800, Napoleon took up his residence in the Tuileries. His salary was five hundred thousand francs a year. Ten days before his removal to the Tuileries, Feb. 9, when the seventy-two flags taken from the Turks at Aboukir were placed in the Hôtel des Invalides, a funeral oration was pronounced on Washington, who had died Dec. 14, 1799. Napoleon issued this order to his army: "Washington is dead! That great man fought against tyranny. He established the liberty of his country. His memory will be ever dear to the freemen of both hemispheres, and especially to the French soldiers, who, like him and the American troops, have fought for liberty and equality. As a mark of respect, the First Consul orders that, for ten days, black crape be suspended from all the standards and banners of the Republic."

Feb. 20 he received a letter from Louis XVIII., in which the Bourbon King said, "Save France from her own violence, and you will fulfil the first wish of my heart. Restore her king to her, and future generations will bless your memory." But Napoleon knew that the French did not want the House of Bourbon. They had put Louis XVI. to death, and still celebrated that anniversary.

Napoleon devoted all his time to the improvement of the state. He drew around him the ablest persons. "The men whom he most disliked," says Bourrienne, "were those whom he called *babblers,* who are continually prating of everything and on everything." He often said, "I want more head and less tongue."

He gave France a new constitution, which was accepted by the votes of the people almost unanimously, over 3,000,000 in the affirmative, and a few hundreds in the negative. He abolished the annual festival celebrating the death of Louis XVI. He opened the prisons where those opposed to the state were confined; hundreds of exiles returned to France. The country was bankrupt; but now that confidence was restored, with the help of the best financiers, the Bank of France was established, a sinking fund provided, judicious taxation adopted, and an era of prosperity began. Napoleon built canals, roads, and bridges, and splendid monuments. He restored Sunday as a day of rest, which had been set aside when the Goddess of Reason was worshipped during the Revolution.

A little later, duly 15, 1801,—by the Concordat,—he recognized the Roman Catholic religion as the religion of France. He said, "I am convinced that a part of France would become Protestant, were I to favor that disposition. I am also certain that the much greater portion would continue Catholic, and that they would oppose, with the greatest zeal, the division among their fellow-citizens. We should then have the Huguenot wars over again, and interminable conflicts. But by reviving a religion which has always prevailed in the country, and by giving perfect liberty of conscience to the minority, all will be satisfied."

He did not like numerous festival days. "A saint's day," he said, "is a day of idleness, and I do not wish for that. People must labor in order to live."

Nobody labored harder than Napoleon. He kept several secretaries busy. Writing fatigued him, and he wrote so hurriedly that the last half of the word was usually a dash, or omitted. He could go without sleep, snatching a few minutes in his chair, or in his saddle before a battle. He seldom took over twenty minutes for dinner, even when he was Emperor, and rose from the table as soon as he had finished. His time was too precious to wait long for others. He was very prompt, and required others to be so.

He said, "Occupation is my element . . . I have seen the extent to which I could use my eyes, but I have never known any bounds to my capacity for application."

Lanfrey says he "had a prodigious power of work," and "a rapidity of conception that no other man has probably ever possessed to the same extent." He used often to say, "Succeed! I judge men only by results."

Nobody knew better the value of time. "I worked all day," said a person to him, in apology for not having completed some duty. "But had you not the night also?" was the reply.

"Ask me for whatever you please except *time*," he said to another; "that is the only thing which is beyond my power."

While taking his bath, Bourrienne read to him. While being shaved, he read, or somebody read to him. He ate fast, and was irregular at his meals, sometimes passing a whole day without eating. He always walked up and down the room, with his arms folded behind him, when dictating to his secretaries. "He was exceedingly temperate," says Bourrienne, "and averse to all excess."

"The institutions of modern France date not, as is often said, from the Revolution, but from the Consulate," says Professor Seeley. "The work of reconstruction which distinguishes the

Consulate, though it was continued under the Empire, is the most enduring of all the achievements of Napoleon."

"The institutions now created," says Seeley, "and which form the organization of modern France, are, 1. The Restored Church, resting on the Concordat; 2. the University; 3. the judicial system; 4. the Codes: *Code Civil*, called *Code Napoléon* Sept. 3, 1807, *Code de Commerce*, *Code Pénal*, *Code d'Instruction Criminelle*; 5. the system of local government; 6. the Bank of France; 7. the Legion of Honor."

"My code will outlive my victories," said Napoleon, truly. He put the best minds of France upon the codification and improvement of her laws, and he carefully watched every detail.

"Bourrienne," Napoleon used to say, "it is for France I am doing all this! All I wish, all I desire, the end of all my labors, is, that my name should be indissolubly connected with that of France!"

Now that France was prosperous and settled, Napoleon wrote to George III., King of England, proposing peace. Lord Grenville, for his nation, which had grown more confident since the battle of the Nile and the successes in Egypt, declined to treat with the Consular Government of France. Canning spoke of this "new usurper, who, like a spectre, wears on his head a something that has a phantom resemblance to a crown." Who would have prophesied then that young Napoleon IV. would have died fighting the battles of England in Zululand?

He proposed peace to Austria, but she decided like her ally, England. Napoleon said bitterly, "England wants war. She shall have it. Yes! yes! war to the death."

He immediately sent General Moreau with one hundred and thirty thousand men against the Austrian army on the Rhine, and took forty thousand himself to Italy, crossing the Alps over the Great St. Bernard. The carriages and wheels were slung on poles; the ammunition boxes were borne on mules; the cannon were carried in trees hollowed out, each dragged up the heights by a hundred men; the soldiers crept up the icy steeps

111

each with sixty or seventy pounds upon his back. At the well-known Hospice kept by the monks, Napoleon had sent forward supplies for his men, who, cold and exhausted, were overjoyed at the repast.

The story is told that the young guide who led Napoleon's mule over the Alps confided to the sympathetic stranger his poverty, his desire to marry the girl of his choice, and his inability to provide her a home. The small man in a gray overcoat gave him a note to the head of the convent. To his astonishment, it provided him with a house and a piece of ground.

The army then swept down upon Italy. The First Consul entered Milan June 2; Lannes was victorious at Montebello June 9, and on the morning of June 14 forty thousand Austrians were opposed to a much smaller number of French on the plain of Marengo. The battle was hotly contested for twelve hours. At first the Austrians seemed victorious, till Desaix, who had just come back from Egypt, rushed upon the field with his reserves. He was shot dead, but his columns were soon avenged.

Six thousand Austrians threw down their arms, a panic spread through their troops, the cavalry plunged over the infantry to be first in crossing the Bormida, and thousands perished in the dreadful confusion. Marengo is regarded by many as Napoleon's most masterful battle.

Desaix's death was a sad blow to Napoleon. Savary found his body stripped of clothing, wrapped it in a cloak, laid it across a horse, and Napoleon had it carried to Milan to be embalmed. He said, "Victory at such a price is dear." Kléber was killed in Egypt on the same day. At St. Helena, Napoleon said, "Of all the generals I ever had under my command, Desaix and Kléber possessed the greatest talent—in particular Desaix . . . Kléber and Desaix were irreparable losses to France."

Napoleon returned to Milan and went in state to the Cathedral to the *Te Deum*, four days after the battle of Marengo. The people everywhere gave him an ovation. "Bourrienne," he said, "do you hear the acclamations still resounding? That noise is as sweet to me as the sound of Josephine's voice." Napoleon reached Paris late in June.

Dec. 3 of this same year, 1800, Moreau fought the famous battle of Hohenlinden, in the black forests of Germany, at midnight. In the blinding snowstorm both armies got entangled in the forests. The Austrians left ten thousand in dead and wounded on the field, with seven thousand prisoners. The poem of Campbell is well known:—

"On Linden, when the sun was low,
All bloodless lay the untrodden snow,
And dark as winter was the flow
Of Iser rolling rapidly."

Finally a treaty of peace between France and Austria was signed at Lunéville, Feb. 9, 1801, followed March 27, 1802, by the treaty of Amiens, between France and England.

Both countries rejoiced in the cessation of hostilities. Fox came over from England and was received with great cordiality. Napoleon said, "I considered him an ornament to mankind, and was very much attached to him."

Four months later, Aug. 4, 1802, by an overwhelming majority of the votes of the people, over three and a half millions in favor to about eight thousand against it, Napoleon was declared Consul for life. La Fayette could not conscientiously favor it, unless liberty of the press were guaranteed. He said to Napoleon, "A free government, and you at its head—that comprehends all my desires."

Napoleon said, "He thinks he is still in the United States— as if the French were Americans. He has no conception of what is required for this country." Napoleon felt, no doubt sincerely, that France was more stable under an Emperor than a President. And yet since the fall of Napoleon III. France has shown that she can live and prosper as a republic.

All through these years the Royalists were plotting to return to the throne; for when did ever a king reign who did not think it was by "Divine right"?

Louis XVIII. wrote another letter to Napoleon: "You must have long since been convinced, General, that you possess my esteem . . . We may insure the glory of France. I say *we*, because I require the aid of Bonaparte, and he can do nothing without me. General, Europe observes you; glory awaits you; I am impatient to restore peace to my people." In answer to this letter, Napoleon wrote, "You must not seek to return to France. To do so, you must trample over a hundred thousand dead bodies."

Several attempts were made to assassinate Napoleon. Possibly some of these were the work of Jacobins, who feared that the republic was slipping into an empire; but they were for the most part traced to Royalists, the leaders of whom lived in England, and were receiving yearly pensions, because they had aided her in former wars.

On the evening of Dec. 24, 1800, as Napoleon was going to the opera to hear Haydn's Oratorio of "The Creation," he was obliged to pass through the Rue Saint-Nicaise, where an upturned cart covered a barrel of gunpowder, grape-shot, and pieces of iron. The "infernal machine" exploded two seconds after he had passed in his carriage. The carriage was uplifted from the ground, four persons were killed, sixty wounded, of whom several died, and forty-six houses were badly damaged. One of the horses of Napoleon's escort was wounded.

Other plans were soon discovered, concocted by Georges Cadoudal, General Pichegru, and others, all in the confidence of the Comte d'Artois, afterwards Charles X., the brother of Louis XVIII. He lived in or near London.

Cadoudal, or Georges as he is usually called, was to meet Napoleon in the streets, and, with a band of thirty or forty followers, kill him and his staff. When all was ready, the Bourbon princes were to be near at hand to head the revolt of the people. Georges was arrested and executed with eleven of his companions.

The Duke d'Enghien, Louis Antoine, Henri de Bourbon, son of the Duke of Bourbon, and a descendant of the great Condé who had done so much for France in her wars, was living at Ettenheim, under the protection of the Margrave of Baden, to be near the lady whom he loved, the Princess Charlotte de Rohan, and "to be ready," says Walter Scott, "to put himself at the head of the royalists in the east of France," if opportunity offered.

It was reported to Napoleon that the duke came over into France probably on political errands, and that he was corresponding with disaffected persons in France.

Napoleon sent some officers to seize the duke on the night of March 15, 1804; he was carried to Strasburg, and thence to the Castle of Vincennes, near Paris, arriving on the afternoon of Tuesday, March 20. He was aroused from sleep a little before six on the morning of the 21st, and innocently asked if he were to be imprisoned. He was conducted outside the castle; by the light of a lantern his sentence was read to him. He denied any complicity in the conspiracy against the life of the First Consul, which was doubtless true; requested to see Napoleon, which was refused; asked an officer to take a ring, a lock of hair, and a letter to his beloved, and was shot at six in the morning, by his open grave, his devoted dog by his side. Bourrienne says, "This faithful animal returned incessantly to the fatal spot . . . The fidelity of the poor dog excited so much interest that the police prevented any one from visiting the fatal spot, and the dog was no longer heard to howl over his master's grave."

Josephine had heard of Napoleon's intention to send terror among the Bourbon conspirators, and had begged him, on her knees and with tears, to save the life of the young prince. It would have been well for him had he listened to her entreaties.

France, and Europe as well, were shocked at this death. The Russian court went into mourning for the Bourbon prince. No doubt Napoleon was incensed by the Bourbon plots, and after this death these ceased; but Las Cases, at St. Helena, said Napoleon always regretted it, saying, "Undoubtedly, if I had been informed in time of certain circumstances respecting the opinions of the prince, and his disposition, if, above all, I had seen the letter which he wrote to me, and which, God knows for what reason, was only delivered to me after his death, I should certainly have forgiven him."

Napoleon has been blamed for another matter,—the taking of Saint Domingo, and the imprisonment of Toussaint L'Ouverture. This remarkable colored man, who had been a slave, had acquired the control of the island by driving the French and Spanish troops out, and making it a republic, with a nominal dependence upon France. Napoleon, with a desire unfortunately shown and carried out by other nations, wished to enlarge his colonies and also to settle some dissensions in the island, and sent Dec. 14, 1801, General Leclerc, who had married his pretty sister Pauline, with 25,000 men to Saint Domingo to re-establish French sovereignty. He was to send back to France any who rebelled. Toussaint L'Ouverture, who was among them, was imprisoned in the fortress of Joux, near Besançon, in Normandy, and died in ten months, away from his own people, the victim of the spirit of conquest, which is not dead even in the nineteenth century. The climate destroyed the French army. Only two or three thousand ever returned. General Leclerc died, like the rest, of yellow fever.

Napoleon said at St. Helena, "I ought to have been satisfied with governing it [Saint Domingo] through the medium of Toussaint . . . The design of reducing it by force was a great error."

Only a year after the treaty of Amiens was concluded, it became evident that it would not last. It was said that Napoleon's power was becoming too great for the security of Europe. England had determined not to give up Malta to the Knights as she had promised. Under Pitt's guidance she was arming and making herself ready for a great combat. The Royalists were using their pens in their English homes, to abuse the head of the French nation, held there by the votes of the French people. It was, of course, exasperating, and tended to produce revolt.

Napoleon called attention to the terms of the treaty, which stipulated that neither of the two nations should give *any protection* to those who were injuring the other. Commercial tariffs bred dislike. English pride was stirred because Napoleon said, "England, single-handed, is unable to cope with France." Finally in May, 1803, the war began. Alison says, and Scott agrees with him, "Upon coolly reviewing the circumstances under which the contest was renewed, it is impossible to deny that the British government manifested a feverish desire to come to a rupture, and that, as far as the transactions between the two countries are concerned, they are the aggressors."

Napoleon was determined to invade England,—Bourrienne thinks it was only a feint, and that his real motive "was to invade Germany and repulse the Russian troops,"—and he gathered an army of 150,000 in and around Boulogne, and an immense flotilla which should be able to transport these men ten leagues across the channel to the English coast.

While these preparations were going on, the French Senate, undoubtedly in accord with the views of the First Consul, suggested publicly the idea of an empire over which Napoleon should be the hereditary ruler. The people were tired of Bourbon plottings, and, if Napoleon were killed, the scenes of the Revolution might again be witnessed in the streets of Paris. Napoleon was declared Emperor of the French, May 18, 1804, and publicly crowned by Pope Pius VII., at Notre Dame, Dec. 2 of the same year.

Paris was thronged with people on the day of the coronation. At half-past ten in the morning Napoleon and Josephine drove to the cathedral in a carriage largely of glass, surmounted by a golden crown upheld by four eagles with outstretched wings, drawn by eight superb horses. Twenty squadrons of cavalry led the procession, Marshal Murat at the head. Eighteen carriages, each drawn by six horses, followed.

Napoleon wore a coat of crimson velvet faced with white velvet, white velvet boots, a short cloak of crimson lined with white satin, and a black velvet cap with two aigrettes and several diamonds.

At the Archbishop's Palace, Napoleon put on his coronation robes. These were a tight-fitting gown of white satin, a crimson mantle covered with golden bees, having an embroidered border with the letter N, and a crown above each letter, the lining and cape of ermine, the whole weighing eighty pounds, and held up by four persons. His crown was of golden laurel; his sword at his left side was in a scabbard of blue enamel, covered with eagles and bees.

Josephine wore a white satin gown, with a train of silver brocade covered with bees, a girdle of very expensive diamonds, necklace, bracelets, and earrings of precious stones and antique cameos, and a diadem of four rows of pearls with clusters of diamonds. The Emperor was much struck with Josephine's beauty, and said to his brother Joseph, "If father could see us!"

As Napoleon entered the cathedral, which was draped in crimson and gold, twenty thousand spectators shouted, "Long live the Emperor!"

The Emperor and Empress knelt on blue velvet cushions before the Pope, who anointed Napoleon on the head and hands, and the Empress in the same way. Then high mass began with three hundred performers. When the moment came for the Pope to crown the Emperor, Napoleon took the crown from his hands and placed it upon his own head, and then crowned Josephine. Her crown was formed of eight branches set in diamonds, emeralds, and amethysts, under a gold globe surmounted by a cross. Then they proceeded to the great throne reached by twenty-four steps, Josephine sitting one step lower than her husband. France had placed her all in the hands of one man; and Lanfrey justly remarks, "A nation that carries love of ease so far as to thrust the whole burden of duties and responsibility on a single man is always punished for it."

After the gorgeous ceremony was over, Napoleon and the Empress dined alone, and were happy. He said to David, who had painted the coronation scene at the moment when Napoleon was placing the crown upon the head of the lovely Josephine, "I thank you for transmitting to ages to come the proof of affection I wanted to give to her who shares with me the pains of government." Then he raised his hat to the artist, and said, "David, I salute you." Josephine had opposed Napoleon's becoming Emperor, because it meant hereditary succession, and she had no child by Napoleon. His brothers had for some years urged a divorce, so that Josephine's life had been one of much sorrow.

Napoleon had said to Bourrienne, "It is the torment of my life not to have a child. I plainly perceive that my power will never be firmly established until I have one. If I die without an heir, not one of my brothers is capable of supplying my place. All is begun, but nothing is ended. God knows what will happen!"

Josephine had urged her young daughter Hortense into a marriage with Louis, the brother of Napoleon, Jan. 2, 1802, with the hope that their child might be the heir to the empire. Each loved another person before marriage, and their married life was one of constant misery.

Their first child, Charles Napoleon, born Oct. 10, 1802, whom Napoleon would have adopted, a beautiful and most intelligent boy, died when he was four years and a half old, of croup, May 5, 1807. "Sometimes when his parents were quarrelling," says Saint-Amand, "he succeeded in reconciling them. He used to take his father by the hand, who gladly let himself be led by this little angel, and then he would say in a caressing tone: 'Kiss her, papa, I beg of you;' then he was perfectly happy when his father and mother exchanged a kiss of peace."

Hortense, the mother, was so prostrated with grief, that it was feared she would lose her reason. Madame de Rémusat says of her, "The Queen has but one thought, the loss she has suffered; she speaks of only one thing, of *him*. Not a tear, but a cold, calm, and almost absolute silence about everything, and when she speaks she wrings every one's heart. If she sees any one whom she has ever seen with her son, she looks at him with kindliness and interest, and says, 'You know he is dead.' When she first saw her mother, she said to her, 'It's not long since he was here with me. I held him on my knees thus.' ... She heard ten o'clock strike; she turned to one of the ladies and said, 'You know it was at ten that he died.' That is the only way she breaks her almost continual silence."

Josephine was doubly crushed by the blow. She saw her hopes for the future blighted. The Emperor wrote to her from the seat of war; "I can well imagine the grief which Napoleon's death must cause. You can understand what I suffer. I should like to be with you, that you might be moderate and discreet in your grief . . . Let me hear that you are calm and well! Do you want to add to my regret? Good-by, my dear."

Napoleon was not cold-hearted, but believed that only those accomplish much in life who have self-control. Two of his soldiers having committed suicide on account of love affairs, Napoleon caused it to be inserted in the order-book of the guard, that "there is as much true courage in bearing up against mental sufferings with constancy as in remaining firm on the wall of a battery."

Nearly six months after the crowning in Notre Dame, the Emperor was crowned King of Italy in the cathedral of Milan, May 26, 1805, with the iron crown of Charlemagne. This crown of gold and precious stones covers an iron ring said to have been made from a spike which pierced the Saviour's hand at the crucifixion. Napoleon and the Empress were both gorgeously arrayed. He placed the crown upon his own head, repeating the words used in ancient times: "God has given it to me—woe to him that touches it."

Everywhere Napoleon and Josephine were adored by the people. They went into the cabin of a poor woman, who was anxious and needy because her husband could not get work. "How much money would make you perfectly happy?" asked Napoleon. "Ah, sir, a great deal! As much as eighty dollars."

The Emperor gave her several hundreds, and told her to rent a piece of ground and buy some goats.

"Josephine," says Saint-Amand, "had all the qualities that are attractive in a sovereign,—affability, gentleness, kindliness, generosity. She had a way of convincing every one of her personal interest. She had an excellent memory, and surprised those with whom she talked by the exactness with which she recalled the past, even to details they had themselves nearly forgotten. The sound of her gentle, penetrating, and sympathetic voice added to the courtesy and charm of her words. Every one listened to her with pleasure; she spoke with grace and listened courteously. She always appeared to be doing a kindness, and thus inspired affection and gratitude."

"Her only fault," says Saint-Amand, "was extravagance." But it must be remembered that Napoleon wished her to dress elegantly. It seemed as though everybody came to ask her to buy, and she bought, says Saint-Amand, "simply to oblige the dealers. There was no limit to her liberality. She would have liked to own all the treasures of the earth in order to give them all away." ... Napoleon, economical by nature, scolded and forgave. "He could refuse Josephine nothing," says the same writer, "and she was really the only woman who had any influence over him."

Napoleon made Josephine's son, Eugène, Viceroy of Italy,— he often said, "Eugène may serve as a model to all the young men of the age,"—returned to Paris, and then started for his troops at Boulogne. There he waited for some days for his feet under Villeneuve, who, having been watched by the English, and in part crippled by them, failed to appear. He dared not proceed to Brest, which the English blockaded, and so repaired to Cadiz, to be crushed soon after by that Napoleon of the sea, Horatio Nelson, at the battle of Trafalgar. Villeneuve afterwards committed suicide, stabbing himself to the heart. He left a letter for his wife in which he said, "What a blessing that I have no children to reap my horrible heritage and bear the weight of my name!"

Meantime, Russia, Austria, and Sweden had joined themselves to England to defeat Napoleon. The Emperor, with that quickness of decision and rapidity of execution for which he was phenomenal, managed to separate the armies of his foes, and beat them in turn. At Ulm, Oct. 20, 1805, over thirty thousand Austrians under General Mack, led by sixteen generals, surrendered, laid down their arms, and retired to the rear of the French army. More than twenty thousand Austrians had been taken prisoners in the few days preceding, and the Austrian army of eighty thousand was well-nigh destroyed.

Napoleon wrote to Josephine Oct. 21: "I am very well, my dear. I have made an army of thirty-three thousand men surrender. I have taken from sixty to seventy thousand prisoners, more than ninety flags, and more than two hundred cannon. In the military annals there is no such defeat."

Napoleon pushed on to Vienna, which he entered Nov. 14, and went to the palace of Schönbrunn. The Emperor Francis had fled, and joined the Tsar and the Russian army at Brunn. Thither Napoleon marched at once. On the night of Dec. 1, 1805, he mounted his horse to reconnoitre the enemy's lines. As he returned, going on foot from one watch-fire to another, he fell to the ground over the stump of a tree. A grenadier lighted a torch of straw, then the whole line did the same and cheered the Emperor. They remembered that the next day, Dec. 2, was the anniversary of the coronation. The Russians thought the French were retreating. Then all slept for a few hours, and awoke to the battle of Austerlitz.

At daybreak there was a heavy mist, then the sun shone out full and clear, and the French believed they would win a glorious victory. They were not disappointed. During the terrible conflict the Russians and Austrians lost over thirty thousand in killed and wounded, treble the number of the French. The enemy fled across the lakes, the ice of which being broken by the French batteries, thousands were ingulfed. Their cries and groans, says Lanfrey, were heard on the following day.

Napoleon said, "I have fought thirty battles like that, but I have never seen so decisive a victory, or one where the chances were so unevenly balanced." The Russian and Austrian forces greatly outnumbered the French. To his soldiers Napoleon said, "I am satisfied with you; you have covered your eagles with undying glory."

To Josephine he wrote: "The battle of Austerlitz is the greatest I have won; forty-five flags, more than one hundred and fifty cannon, the standards of the Russian guards, twenty generals, more than twenty thousand killed,—a horrid sight! The Emperor Alexander is in despair, and is leaving for Russia. Yesterday I saw the Emperor of Germany in my bivouac; we talked for two hours, and agreed on a speedy peace . . . I shall see with pleasure the time that will restore me to you."

The defeat of the allies at Austerlitz hastened the death of William Pitt of England. He looked long on the map of Europe, and said, "Henceforth we may close that map for half a century." He died Jan. 23, 1806.

On Napoleon's return to Paris he erected a column in the Place Vendôme to the Grand Army. It was constructed of cannon taken from the enemy, and has illustrations upon it of the campaigns of Ulm and Austerlitz. W. O'Connor Morris calls Austerlitz "the most perfect of battles on land, as the Nile was the most perfect on sea." Seeley thinks, in its historical results, Austerlitz "ranks among the great events of the world."

The peace of Pressburg was effected between France and Austria, Dec. 26, 1805. Charles James Fox, who had succeeded Pitt in England, was favorable to peace between the nations, but the war party in England was strong. Fox soon died, and the peace negotiations failed.

Napoleon said at St. Helena, "The death of Fox was one of the fatalities of my career. Had his life been prolonged, affairs would have taken a totally different turn. The cause of the people would have triumphed, and we should have established a new order of things in Europe."

Meantime Napoleon had placed his brother Joseph on the throne of Naples, Louis on the throne of Holland, and had formed a Confederation of the Rhine out of several states in the valley of the Rhine, which had fourteen million people. Napoleon was elected Protector of the Confederation.

Russia now became an ally of Prussia, and war was declared against France Oct. 14, 1806. The double battle of Jena and Auerstädt was fought, and the Prussians were completely defeated. Alison says, "The loss of the Prussians was prodigious; on the two fields there fell nearly twenty thousand killed and wounded, besides nearly as many prisoners . . . Ten thousand of the killed and wounded fell at Auerstädt."

Napoleon entered Berlin in triumph Oct. 27, 1806, and established himself in the king's palace. He did not like the beautiful Queen Louise, because he felt that she had inspired the soldiers by her presence, and urged her husband to make war. He was unjust to her in his bulletins, and Josephine reproached him for "speaking ill of women."

Napoleon visited the palace of Sans Souci to see the room where Frederick the Great died, still preserved as he left it, and then went to the church where he is buried. At the tomb, says General de Ségur, "Napoleon paused at the entrance in a grave and respectful attitude. He gazed into the shadow enclosing the hero's ashes, and stood thus for nearly ten minutes, motionless, silent, as if buried in deep thought." The sword of Frederick he took with him, and gave it to the Hotel des Invalides in Paris, with the flags carried by his guard in the Seven Years' War.

Early in November, Prince Hohenlohe surrendered twenty thousand Prussians to the French; and Blücher, whom Napoleon was to meet again at Waterloo, surrendered twenty thousand men and over five hundred officers.

With all this victory, Josephine was not happy. Napoleon wrote her Nov. 1: "Talleyrand has come, and tells me you do nothing but cry." She wrote to Hortense, more miserable than herself, that she could not be happy so far from the Emperor.

Napoleon, while at Berlin, issued, Nov. 21, 1806, his famous "Berlin Decree," wherein he declared the British Islands blockaded. All commerce with England and her colonies was prohibited; all property belonging to an English subject confiscated; every native of England found in a country occupied by French troops to be made prisoner of war.

Napoleon declared that this was a retaliatory measure against England. Every French port was, in fact, blockaded by English vessels from the Elbe to Brest, by a decree of the British Government, passed in May, 1806, according to Alison. Some months after the Berlin Decree, England issued further prohibitory acts, called Orders in Council. The consequence of all this was that hate between the two nations was increased.

After the humiliation of Prussia, the war went on with Russia. After some minor battles, both armies met on the bloody field of Eylau, Feb. 7, 1807. Jomini thinks the forces about equal, though some historians place the number at eighty thousand Russians, and sixty thousand French. Part of Feb. 7 and all of Feb. 8, the armies were in deadly conflict. A blinding snowstorm part of the time prevented the armies from seeing each other. The snow and ice were so thick that men fought on ponds and did not know it.

Fifty thousand dead and wounded lay on the snow. Marshal Augereau's corps was almost destroyed; three thousand only remained out of fifteen thousand. Napoleon wrote in his bulletins: "Imagine, on a space a league square, nine or ten thousand corpses; four or five thousand dead horses; lines of Russian knapsacks; fragments of guns and sabres; the earth covered with bullets, shells, supplies; twenty-four cannon surrounded by their artillerymen, slain just as they were trying to take their guns away; and all that in plainest relief on the stretch of snow."

He said, as he looked upon the ghastly field, "This sight is one to fill rulers with a love of peace and a horror of war." At three o'clock in the morning of Feb. 9, he wrote to Josephine:

"We had a great battle yesterday. I was victorious, but our loss was heavy; that of the enemy, which was even greater, is no consolation for me. I write you these few lines myself, though I am very tired, to tell you that I am well and love you.

Ever yours."

Baron de Marbot, in his most interesting memoirs, tells of his thrilling experiences in this battle. He was at that time an officer under Augereau. His horse, Lisette, of whom he was extremely fond, was addicted to biting, but valued for her speed. At great risk, Marbot carried a message to the Fourteenth. "I see no means of saving the regiment," said the major; "return to the Emperor, bid him farewell from the Fourteenth of the line, which has faithfully executed his orders, and bear him the eagle which he gave us, and which we can no longer defend; it would add too much to the pain of death to see it fall into the hands of the enemy."

Marbot took the eagle, when a cannon ball went through the hinder part of his hat, forcing, by the shock, the blood from his nose, ears, and even eyes. His limbs were almost paralyzed. A hand to hand combat raged around him. Several Frenchmen, not to be struck from behind, set their backs against the sides of Lisette, who stood quite still. One of the Russians thrust his bayonet into Marbot's left arm, and then into Lisette's thigh.

"Her ferocious instincts being restored by the pain," says Marbot, "she sprang at the Russian, and at one mouthful tore off his nose, lips, eyebrows, and all the skin of his face, making of him a living death's-head, dripping with blood. Then, hurling herself with fury among the combatants, kicking and biting, Lisette upset everything that she met on the road."

She seized another Russian who had tried to hit Marbot, "tore out his entrails, and mashed his body under her feet, leaving him dying on the snow."

When Lisette and her rider reached the cemetery of Eylau, where the battle was hottest, the poor creature fell exhausted. The young Marbot, supposed to be dead amid the piles of dead and wounded, was stripped of his clothing. He was marvellously rescued by a servant, who cut up the shirt of a dead soldier and bandaged the leg of Lisette, by which she also was saved. Lisette, after doing service just before Friedland by galloping twelve leagues on a hot day to carry a message of warning to the Emperor, was cared for by the wife of an officer, and died of old age.

Napoleon shared with his soldiers all the dangers and privations of war. He wrote to his brother Joseph: "The staff-officers have not taken off their clothes for two months, and some not for four. I have myself been a fortnight without taking off my boots. We are deep in the snow and mud . . . The wounded have to be carried in open sleighs for fifty leagues."

Josephine wished to come to him. He wrote: "You couldn't be racing through inns and camps. I am as anxious as you can be to see you and be quiet . . . All my life I have sacrificed everything—peace, interest, happiness—to my destiny."

The next great battle was at Friedland, when eighty thousand French met seventy-five thousand Russians. "This is the anniversary of Marengo," said Napoleon, June 14, 1800, "and to-day *fortune is with me.*"

And so it proved. The Russians fought desperately, but they were overpowered. They retreated towards the river, and thousands who were not captured were drowned. They lost twenty-six thousand, says Marbot, in dead and wounded, and the French about half that number.

The conquered were glad to make peace, which was concluded at Tilsit, July 7, 1807, between Alexander I. of Russia, Frederick William III. of Prussia, and Napoleon. By this treaty, among other articles, some provinces west of the Elbe were made into the kingdom of Westphalia, and another brother of Napoleon, Jerome, was placed upon a throne. He had married, when nineteen, Miss Elizabeth Patterson of Baltimore; but through Napoleon's influence the union was annulled, and he married, at twenty-three, Aug. 23, 1807, the daughter of the king of Würtemberg. She proved a noble woman. When her husband was dethroned in 1814, she refused to obtain a divorce, writing to her father: "Having been forced, by reasons of state, to marry the king, my husband, it has been granted me by fate to be the happiest woman in the world."

Napoleon said of her at Saint Helena, "Princess Catherine of Würtemberg has, with her own hands, written her name in history."

Napoleon returned to Paris after the peace of Tilsit, and was received with unbounded love and honor. He made Paris more beautiful with arches and churches, he developed her industries, and he established schools and colleges. He said, "We must not pass through this world without leaving traces which may commend our memory to posterity."

England was still the bitter enemy of Napoleon. The decrees of both regarding commerce were soon to plunge nearly all Europe into war. By agreement of Alexander and Napoleon, if England did not consent to peace, they were to summon Denmark, Sweden, Portugal, and perhaps Austria, to close their ports against her. Denmark wished to be neutral. While she hesitated, England, having heard of this project, sent a fleet against Copenhagen and bombarded it.

Napoleon sent an army under Junot into Portugal to compel her assent, and Murat into Spain, which at that time was friendly with France, though distracted by royal dissensions. Napoleon placed his brother Joseph on the throne. Mr. Ropes thinks, and probably correctly, that Napoleon supposed "the population of the Spanish peninsula was ready for the great reforms in government in which France had led the way, and in which Holland, Western Germany, and Italy were then cheerfully and hopefully marching, and that the better and more enlightened part of the Spanish people would be thankful to see a liberal, intelligent, and conscientious man like Joseph take the place of the bigoted and profligate Charles IV."

Napoleon said at St. Helena: "It was the subject of my perpetual dreams to render Paris the real capital of Europe . . . My ambition was of the highest and noblest kind that ever existed,—that of establishing and consecrating the empire of reason, and the full exercise and complete enjoyment of all the human faculties."

A dreadful insurrection took place in Spain against the rule of Joseph, and Napoleon sent a large army to quell it. He succeeded in reinstating Joseph on the throne for a time. He abolished the Inquisition and began several reforms.

The insurrection in Spain gave great joy in England. "The general rapture knew no bounds," says Alison. England sent her armies into Spain and Portugal, and the Peninsular War resulted, which Napier has described so vividly. To restore Ferdinand, the son of Charles IV., to Spain, England spent, says Napier, one hundred millions sterling, about five hundred million dollars, "and the bones of forty thousand British soldiers lie scattered on the plains and mountains of the Peninsula." The heroic Sir John Moore fell at Corunna, and was buried in his bloody cloak at night by torchlight.

> "Not a drum was heard, not a funeral note,
> As his corse to the ramparts we hurried;
> Not a soldier discharged his farewell shot
> O'er the grave where our hero we buried."

His last words were, "I hope the people of England will be satisfied. I hope my country will do me justice." After his death, Sir Arthur Wellesley, the Duke of Wellington, was made commander-in-chief of all the English troops in the Spanish peninsula. Austria considered this an opportune time to make war on Napoleon. The latter raised another immense army,— Lanfrey says with much truth, "France was bleeding to death,"—

marched against Austria, and several bloody battles resulted.

At Eckmühl the Austrians, says Marbot, admitted a loss of five thousand killed, and fifteen thousand prisoners. Napoleon said at St. Helena, "The greatest military manœuvres I ever made, and those for which I give myself most credit, were performed at Eckmühl."

At Ratisbon the Emperor was wounded in the foot, just before the retaking. So wild were the soldiers at the news, that as soon as his wound was dressed he rode in front of the whole line to appease their anxiety.

After some other successes, Napoleon reached Vienna, May 10, the Emperor Francis having fled, as before, to a place of safety. Napoleon went at once to the royal palace of Schönbrunn.

The enemy were now on the left bank of the Danube. The spring rains had swollen the great river, and the crossing was most hazardous. In the midst of the thousand yards of water was the huge Island of Lobau, four and a half miles long. Here the troops of Napoleon intrenched themselves, and built a bridge of boats to either side of the Danube. As soon as a portion of the French troops had crossed the river, and reached the towns of Aspern and Essling, the Austrians fell upon them with great slaughter, compelling the French to retreat to the Island of Lobau, in the middle of the river. In these battles the heroic Lannes had both legs crushed by a cannon-ball. One leg was amputated. The Emperor knelt beside the stretcher and wept as he embraced Lannes, whose blood stained Napoleon's white kerseymere waistcoat.

"You will live, my friend, you will live," said the Emperor.

"I trust I may, if I can still be of use to France and your Majesty," was the reply.

After his death, said Marbot, "Napoleon embraced the marshal's body, bathing it with tears, and saying repeatedly, 'What a loss for France and for me!'"

The losses at this double battle are variously estimated from twenty to fifty thousand; Lanfrey accepts the latter number.

Seeley calls it "one of the most terrible and bloody battles of the period." Napoleon at once began to build substantial bridges on piles across the Danube, one of them eight hundred yards long, broad enough for three carriages to pass abreast. These bridges were finished in twenty days, and compelled great admiration.

To the astonishment of the Austrians, he crossed most of his army of 150,000 men during the night of July 4, and on July 6 fought the dreadful battle of Wagram. About 300,000 were in the battle. Fifty thousand on both sides were killed and wounded, probably about an equal number in each army.

The weather was extremely hot, and the corn on the battle-field caught fire from the shells. "The movements of both armies were hampered by the necessity of avoiding it," says Marbot; "for if once troops were overtaken by it, pouches and wagons exploded, carrying destruction through the ranks . . . Of the soldiers who were severely wounded, great numbers perished in the flames; and of those whom the fire did not reach, many lay for days hidden by the tall corn, living during that time on the ears. The Emperor had the plains searched by bands of cavalry, and vehicles were brought from Vienna to remove the wounded, friends and foes alike. But few of those even whom the fire had passed recovered, and the soldiers had a saying that straw-fire had killed nearly as many as gun-fire."

"After the battle," says General Savary, "the Emperor sent sixty francs in crown pieces to each wounded soldier, and more than this to each officer."

Oct. 14, 1809, the peace of Vienna was signed at Schönbrunn, between France and Austria. "I committed a great fault after the battle of Wagram," said Napoleon at St. Helena, "in not reducing the power of Austria still more. She remained too strong for our safety, and to her we must attribute our ruin."

On Napoleon's return to France he had made up his mind to an act which will always tarnish his fame, and from which the decadence of his empire may be dated. He would divorce Josephine, and marry another, with the hope that he might have an heir to the throne. Undoubtedly he believed he was doing the best thing for France; and Thiers says the French people, while they loved Josephine, wished for the divorce.

On Nov. 30, 1809, as he and Josephine were dining together at Fontainebleau, not a word having been uttered except Napoleon asked one of the servants what time it was, he communicated to her his decision. After dismissing the servants, he came to her, took her hand, pressed it to his heart, and said, "Josephine! my dear Josephine! You know how I have loved you . . . To you, to you alone, I owe the only moments of happiness I have tasted in this world. But, Josephine, my destiny is not to be controlled by my will. My dearest affections must yield to the interests of France."

"I expected this," said poor Josephine, "but the blow is none the less mortal."

She became at once insensible; and Napoleon, alarmed, hastily called assistance and bore her to her room. He came to see her in the evening, and wept.

Eugène determined at once to resign his position as Viceroy of Italy, but his mother begged him to remain the friend of Napoleon.

On Dec. 15, at the Tuileries, before the officers of the Empire, the divorce was announced. Josephine was almost overcome by her sobs. "The Emperor will always find in me his best friend," she said, and so it proved.

The next day the divorce was consummated before the Senate. Eugène announced the divorce, saying, "The tears of the Emperor do honor to my mother." Josephine, in a simple white muslin dress, leaning on the arm of Hortense, entered and signed the fatal decree. Both mother and daughter were in tears, as well as many of those present. Eugène, who idolized his mother, fell fainting to the floor. That evening when Josephine thought her husband had retired, she came to his room, her eyes swollen with weeping, and tottering towards the bed fell upon his neck, and sobbed as though her heart would break. They wept together, and talked for an hour. The next day Napoleon came to see her, accompanied by his secretary, Meneval. "He pressed her to his bosom with the most ardent embraces," says Meneval. "In the excess of her emotion she fainted."

At eleven o'clock the same day, veiled from head to foot, Josephine entered a close carriage drawn by six horses, said good-by to the Tuileries forever, and was driven to Malmaison. She retained the title of Empress, with $600,000 a year for her support. Napoleon passed eight days in retirement at Trianon. On his return to the Tuileries, he wrote to her, "I have been very lonely . . . This great palace appears to me empty, and I find myself in solitude. Adieu, my love."

He frequently visited Malmaison. One day he found Josephine painting a violet. She says, "He threw himself with transport into the arms of his old friend . . . It seemed impossible for him to cease gazing upon me, and his look was that of the most tender affection. At length he said, 'My dear Josephine, I have always loved you. I love you still. Do you still love me?'"

Three months later, Mar. 11, 1810, Napoleon was married by proxy at Vienna, Archduke Charles representing him at the wedding, to Marie Louise, the daughter of Emperor Francis I. of Austria. He met her with his suite at the palace of Compiègne. She was eighteen, with light hair, and blue eyes, and gentle in manner. Napoleon was forty.

The civil marriage was celebrated at St. Cloud, April 1; and the next day they made their triumphal entry into Paris, by the Arc de l'Étoile, to the Tuileries, amid the cheers of three hundred thousand people. The world must have been amazed at such a union of France and Austria,—nations which had been at war for years. No wonder Napoleon, at St. Helena, spoke of it as "an abyss covered with a bed of flowers."

Two weeks later Josephine wrote him, "Your majesty shall never be troubled in his happiness by an expression of my grief. I offer incessant prayers that your majesty may be happy."

A year after his marriage, Mar. 20, 1811, a son, Napoleon Francis, was born to Napoleon, called the King of Rome, as the Roman States had been annexed to the Empire. All France rejoiced when the firing of one hundred guns announced the event.

Josephine wrote at once, telling Napoleon, "More than any one in the world do I rejoice in your joy." Of Marie Louise she wrote, "She cannot be more tenderly devoted to you than I am, but she has been enabled to contribute more toward your happiness, by securing that of France . . . Not till you have ceased to watch by her bed, not till you are weary of embracing your son, will you take your pen to converse with your best friend. I will wait."

Napoleon brought his child to Josephine. "The moment I saw you enter," she wrote him, "bearing the young Napoleon in your hands, was unquestionably one of the happiest of my life."

He said at St. Helena: "Josephine would willingly have seen Marie Louise. She frequently spoke of her with great interest . . . Marie Louise manifested the utmost dislike, and even jealousy, of Josephine. I wished one day to take her to Malmaison, but she burst into tears when I made the proposal. She said she did not object to my visiting Josephine, only she did not wish to know it. But whenever she suspected my intention of going to Malmaison, there was no stratagem which she did not employ for the sake of annoying me."

The emperor was devoted to his son, and always considerate and tender to Marie Louise. The boy developed into a very beautiful and bright child, winning the love of everybody.

A little more than a year after the birth of the King of Rome, Russia and France were again at war. Whatever Alexander's personal feelings toward Napoleon, his nobles were opposed to him; they disliked his restrictions on commerce, and feared his growing power. Russia and England became allies, though Napoleon offered to make peace with the latter, which offers she always declined. Probably the real truth was they all wished to humble Napoleon.

Russia and France each raised a great army, the latter about a half million men.

Napoleon left Paris for Dresden, May 9, taking Marie Louise with him. He left her at Prague. Before he started from Paris he spent two hours in earnest conversation with Josephine at Malmaison.

This Grand Army must have made an imposing appearance, with their twenty thousand carriages, one hundred and eighty thousand horses employed in the artillery, besides thousands of provision wagons and baggage.

He began to cross the river Niemen, which empties into the Baltic, on the night of June 23, 1812. The policy of the Russians was to retreat, burning the towns through which they passed, and destroying all produce, that the French might find no support in the desolated country.

The first terrible battle was at Borodino, Sept. 7, where the French lost about thirty thousand, and the Russians fifty thousand, in killed and wounded.

On Sept. 14, Napoleon and his weary army—many thousands had been stationed at various places along the route—entered Moscow. Here they hoped for food and rest. They found the great city deserted. Powder had been placed under the Kremlin, and shells under the larger palaces, where Napoleon and his officers would be apt to lodge; water-pipes had been cut, fountains destroyed; and, the day after Napoleon's arrival, the whole city was set on fire by Russians detailed for that purpose. No wonder Napoleon said, years later, of this terrible destruction of a great city, "It was the most grand, the most sublime, the most terrific sight the world ever beheld!"

Napoleon wrote to the Tsar proposing peace; but no answer was ever returned, though he waited some weeks in Moscow, hoping to hear favorably. The more intelligent serfs offered to rise against their masters, and aid Napoleon, but he did not desire civil war.

On Oct. 19, 1812, the Grand Army of France, one hundred thousand strong, commenced its heart-breaking retreat. Deep snow had already come, earlier than usual. Kutusof, the Russian general, moved his army parallel to the French, and fought them at every available point. Marshal Ney covered the rear, and made for himself an immortal record. Napoleon rightly called him "The Bravest of the Brave." When they reached Borodino they sadly turned their heads away from the battle-fields where the bodies of thirty thousand men were half devoured by wolves. The cold became intense. Horses slipped and fell on the icy ground. Artillery and baggage were abandoned. There was no food in the devastated country. Where Napoleon had left provisions on his way to Moscow the enemy had destroyed them. Men ate their horses for food. They lay down at night on the snow to sleep, and never rose. "Every morning," says Marbot, "we left thousands of dead in our bivouacs . . . So intense was the cold that we could see a kind of vapor rising from men's ears and eyes. Condensing, on contact with the air, this vapor fell back on our persons with a rattle such as grains of millet might have made. We had often to halt and clear away from the horses' bits the icicles formed by their frozen breath . . . Many soldiers of all ranks blew out their brains to put an end to their misery . . . All ranks were confounded; there were no arms, no military bearings; soldiers, officers, generals, were clad in rags, and for boots had nothing but strips of leather or cloth, hardly fastened together with a string." The Emperor himself was grave, calm, and self-controlled, with no diminution of courage.

The soldiers of the allies of Napoleon, Austria, Prussia, Spain, and others, deserted by the thousands, the Russians having sent proclamations in various languages into the camps, telling them they should be returned to their homes.

Finally they reached the river Beresina, the bridge over which had been destroyed by the Russians. Tearing down the hovels in the village, the French built two bridges at night, the men standing for six or seven hours in the water. Then the troops surged upon them, and one bridge broke under the weight of guns and men. In rushing upon the other, great crowds were forced into the river and drowned. The Russians meantime swept them with cannon. From twenty to twenty-five thousand men perished in this dreadful crossing of the Beresina.

On Dec. 5, 1812, they were within the borders of Poland; and Napoleon, having learned that his death had been proclaimed in Paris, and that a man had tried to usurp the power, left his army in charge of Murat, and, with two officers, hastened by sledges to Paris, which he reached Dec. 18.

The loss of the French army and its allies in the Russian campaign Thiers estimates as 300,000 men; other authorities make it 350,000; 100,000 were killed in the advance and retreat from Moscow; 150,000 died of hunger, fatigue, and cold; 100,000 were taken prisoners. The Russian losses were also heavy.

Prussia now joined herself to Russia, and declared war against France. Napoleon at once raised another army of nearly two hundred thousand by conscription, and defeated the enemy at Lützen, or Gross-Beeren, and Bautzen. His young conscripts fought heroically. His beloved Marshal Duroc was killed just after the latter battle. Napoleon wept as he left him dying, saying, "Duroc, there is another life . . . We shall one day meet again."

Austria offered to be a mediator, but failing, hastened to join Prussia and Russia. The marriage with Marie Louise had not won Napoleon friends, as he had fondly hoped.

The allies now had five hundred thousand men, the Prussians under Blücher, the Austrians under Schwarzenberg. Upon Aug. 27, 1813, Napoleon defeated them at Dresden, where they left forty thousand on the field, half of whom were prisoners, but was himself defeated in the dreadful battle of Leipsic, Oct. 16-19.

Bavaria and Westphalia had been compelled to join the allies, whose forces thrice outnumbered the French. The Swedes, under Bernadotte, had now turned against France. "In the three days' battle," says Alison, "the French lost 60,000 men, and the allies nearly as many."

In the retreat of the French from Leipsic they were obliged to cross the Elster river. The bridge had been mined, and by a mistake was exploded before all the French had passed over.

Marbot says, of those who were left in Leipsic, about 13,000 were killed, and 25,000 made prisoners.

Meantime the English had been victorious over the French in Spain and Portugal, and Joseph Bonaparte had been driven from the throne. He came to the United States and lived at Bordentown, New Jersey, for some years, dying at Florence, Italy, July 28, 1844, at the age of seventy-six.

The allies now pushed into France, determined to enter Paris and dethrone Napoleon. The Emperor raised a new army, and with prodigious energy and courage fought against the coalition of Europe. Often with his forces greatly inferior in number to the allies, he defeated them, but finally he was overborne. Marie Louise fled to Blois. The young King of Rome refused to go. "They are betraying my papa," he said, "and I will not go away. I do not wish to leave the palace." He wept as he was taken to the carriage. His governess promised that he should come back, but she was never able to keep her promise.

Paris capitulated March 30, 1814; and the Senate, through the lead of Talleyrand, declared that Napoleon and his family had forfeited the throne.

Napoleon arrived at Paris a few hours after the capitulation, stunned at the news. Fearless as ever, he wished to attack the allies, but was persuaded by his marshals to desist.

With agony of soul, but calmness of demeanor, he signed his abdication at Fontainebleau, April 6, 1814: "The Emperor Napoleon declares that he renounces, for himself and his heirs, the throne of France and Italy; and that there is no personal sacrifice, not even that of life itself, which he is not willing to make for the interests of France."

By the will of the allies, Louis XVIII. was recalled, and Napoleon was banished to the Island of Elba, east of Corsica, with an annual income from France of $500,000. He bade the Old Guard an affectionate good-by. "Adieu, my children," he said. "I would that I could press you all to my heart. Let me at least embrace your general and your eagle." He put his arms around General Petit, and kissed the eagle on its silver beak. Amid the tears and sobs of his brave soldiers, on April 20, Napoleon drove away from Fontainebleau to Fréjus, and in the British frigate, The Undaunted, set sail for Elba, April 27, 1814.

He had frequently written to Josephine through these melancholy months. Once he wrote: "To me death would now be a blessing. But I would once more see Josephine," and he saw her before his departure.

Four days before he left Fontainebleau for Elba, he wrote, "Adieu, my dear Josephine. Be resigned, as I am, and never forget him who never forgot, and who never will forget you. Farewell, Josephine."

She longed to follow him to Elba, but waited to see if Marie Louise would join him. At first Marie Louise desired to go to him, but was prevailed upon by her father, the Emperor Francis, to return to Austria, where she and her son became virtually prisoners. She finally retired to the Duchy of Parma, which the allies had given her, and later married her chamberlain, Count de Neipperg, an Austrian general.

Josephine wrote to Napoleon: "I have been on the point of quitting France to follow your footsteps, and to consecrate to you the remainder of an existence which you so long embellished. A single motive restrains me, and that you may divine . . . Say but the word, and I depart."

As soon as Napoleon went to Elba, Josephine's health rapidly declined. She caught cold in driving in the park at Malmaison. When near death she said to Hortense, "I can say with truth, in this, my dying hour, that the first wife of Napoleon never caused a single tear to flow."

Napoleon landed at Elba, May 4, 1814. A month later, May 29, Josephine died, uttering, with her last breath, "Napoleon! Elba!"

"I have seen," said Mademoiselle Avrillon, the first lady of her bedchamber, "the Empress Josephine's sleeplessness and her terrible dreams. I have known her to pass whole days buried in the gloomiest thought. I know what I have seen and heard, and I am sure that grief killed her!"

Napoleon's mother, a woman of sixty-four, and his sister Pauline, joined him at Elba. The latter had married Prince Borghese in 1803, but they soon separated. After several years they were reconciled to each other. She died at Florence in 1825. Napoleon remained at Elba ten months, when he escaped, landed at Cannes, Mar. 1, 1815, raised an army in France as if by magic, and entered Paris at its head, Mar. 20.

The people seemed glad to be rid of Louis XVIII., who fled at midnight, Mar. 19. Napoleon said, with much truth, "The Bourbons, during their exile, had learned nothing, and forgotten nothing." The Grand Army joyously received their leader. The people shouted themselves hoarse. They wept, and sang songs of thanksgiving. Paris was brilliant with illuminations. When he reached the Tuileries, he was seized and borne aloft above the heads of the throng. The ladies of the court, says Alison, "received him with transports, and imprinted fervent kisses on his cheeks, his hands, and even his dress. Never was such a scene witnessed in history." Hortense and her two children were at the Tuileries to welcome Napoleon.

The allies cared little whom France wished to rule her. They preferred the conservative Bourbons or indeed anybody who would not disturb the so-called balance of power in Europe. They at once banded themselves together, England, Austria, Russia, Prussia, Portugal, Spain, and Sweden, to crush this "enemy and disturber of the world."

A million men were soon raised by the allies, and Napoleon brought together over 200,000. He decided at once to take the offensive rather than let the allies invade France. He left Paris for Belgium, June 12, 1815, taking with him about 120,000 men. He drove the Prussians out of Charleroi, and on June 16 gained a victory over the Prussian marshal, Blücher, at Ligny. Jomini, who is usually authentic, says Napoleon had 72,000 in the battle, and Blücher from 80,000 to 90,000. It was a hotly contested battle-field in which the Prussians lost from 12,000 to 20,000 men. Thiers says 30,000.

Blücher had his gray charger, given him by the Prince Regent of England, shot under him, and was nearly killed in the retreat. The same day occurred the desperate battle of Quatre-Bras, in which Marshal Ney was defeated.

On June 18, 1815, the decisive battle of Waterloo was fought, nine miles south-east of Brussels. Napoleon's forces, according to Jomini and Thiers, were 70,000 in number; Seeley and Ropes say 72,000. Wellington had about 68,000.

The ground was so drenched by rains that the battle was not begun till a little past eleven. Both sides fought desperately. Blücher, a few miles to the right of Wellington, at Wavre, had promised to join him. Napoleon had told Marshal Grouchy to follow the Prussians and thus prevent their union with the English. He started too late for Wavre; he did not take the advice of some of his officers to hasten to Napoleon when they heard the sound of battle, and his 33,000 men failed to help at Waterloo. Ropes gives an interesting account of this in the *Atlantic Monthly*, June, 1881, "Who lost Waterloo?"

All day long the battle raged. Hand to hand combats were constant. The battle seemed in favor of the French. Meantime Blücher was coming from Wavre, with his guns sinking axle-deep in the mud. "We shall never get on," was heard on all sides. "We *must get on*," said the bluff Blücher; "I have given my word to Wellington."

Napoleon kept watching for Grouchy. Early in the afternoon about 30,000 Prussians under Bulow had come to Wellington's assistance. Night came on and the firing of musketry was heard. "There's Grouchy!" said the Emperor. His aide-de-camp, Labédoyère, rushed to announce it to the army. "Marshal Grouchy is arriving, the Guard is going to charge. Courage! courage! 'tis all over with the English."

"One last shout of hope burst from every rank," says M. Fleury de Chaboulon, ex-secretary of the Emperor; "the wounded who were still capable of taking a few steps returned to the combat, and thousands of voices eagerly repeated, Forward! forward!"

It was not Grouchy, but Blücher with thirty or forty thousand fresh troops. The Imperial Guard did indeed charge with all their wonted impetuosity. They were mowed down like grain. Ney, with five horses shot under him, marched on foot with his drawn sword. Napoleon watched them, pale, yet calm. "All is lost!" said he, "the Guard recoils!"

The Emperor was everywhere in the battle. "Death shuns you. You will be made a prisoner," said his generals, and an officer seized the bridle of his horse and dragged him away.

The French were completely overcome, and the Prussians pursued them with great vigor. It is estimated that the French lost thirty thousand on the field of Waterloo, and the loss of the allies was probably not much less. It was one of the most bloody battles of modern times.

Napoleon returned to Paris, and then retired to Malmaison. He abdicated in favor of his son, Napoleon II.; but the allies, when they captured Paris a second time, July 7, 1815, placed Louis XVIII. again on the throne.

Napoleon repaired to Rochefort with the hope that he might embark for America, but the coast was so blockaded by the English steamers that this was impossible. He surrendered himself to go on board the English ship, Bellerophon, July 15, with the hope that he should find a generous foe. He soon learned, to his inexpressible grief, that he was destined for St. Helena. On Aug. 7 he was transferred to the Northumberland, and sailed for his lonely place of exile, which he reached Oct. 16, 1815.

The Island of St. Helena, ten miles broad and seven long, is in the Atlantic Ocean, fourteen hundred miles west of the west coast of South Africa. It is composed of rugged mountains of volcanic origin, with little vegetation. Wherever a vessel could approach a fort was planted, so that the island formed a complete prison.

Lieutenant John R. Glover, who accompanied the British

admiral who took Napoleon to St. Helena, said of the island (*Century*, for November, 1893): "Nothing can possibly be less prepossessing, nay, more horribly forbidding, than the first appearance of this isolated and apparently burnt up barren rock, which promises neither refreshment nor pleasure . . . During our eight months' residence we experienced little variation, and had continued rains. The climate is by no means healthy, ... the children being sickly, and the adults suffering from the liver, of which complaint many of our men died."

Here Napoleon lived for six years, till his death, May 5, 1821, at the age of fifty-two, of a cancer in the stomach, the same disease which had killed his father. He was allowed to take with him to St. Helena three of his generals and their families, and a secretary, Las Cases.

His jailer, Sir Hudson Lowe, seems to have been a most unfortunate choice in the surveillance of a high-spirited and remarkable man.

Napoleon was allowed to walk or ride only within certain limits, with a British officer near at hand. His accommodations were poor and plain. "The rats," says Dr. O'Meara, "are in numbers almost incredible. I have frequently seen them assemble like broods of chickens round the offal thrown out of the kitchen." Besides he says, through the roof "the rain entered in torrents." Napoleon's letters were all opened, both those sent or received. He was never addressed as Emperor, England ungenerously insisting that he be called simply General Bonaparte. Books addressed to "The Emperor" were not delivered to him. William O'Connor Morris says: "His humiliation was degrading and needless . . . Admitting that the allies had a right to deprive him of liberty, they had no right to subject him to insult and wrong; and St. Helena is a blot on the fair fame of England." From his idolized son he was not permitted to hear.

He said to Countess Montholon, at St. Helena, "On receiving into my arms that infant, so many times fervently implored of Heaven, could I have believed that one day he would have become the source of my greatest anguish? Yes, madame, every day he costs me tears of blood. I imagine to myself the most horrid events, which I cannot remove from my mind. I see either the potion or the empoisoned fruit which is about to terminate the days of that young innocent by the most cruel sufferings."

The boy worshipped his father. "Tell him," said the little King of Rome, then four years old, when Meneval, Napoleon's former secretary, left Marie Louise in Austria, "that I love him dearly." He looked like his father, had his ambition, and, as he grew to manhood, longed to return to France. When Charles X. was overthrown in 1830, he said, "Why was I not there to take my chance?" He was then nineteen. Napoleon had foreseen the fall of the Bourbons, as he said at St. Helena, "They will not maintain their position after my death; a reaction in my favor will take place everywhere, even in England."

Napoleon II. died at Vienna, July 22, 1832, at the age of twenty-one, of consumption, at Schönbrunn, the summer home of the Emperor. He expired upon the same narrow bed on which his father slept when he came as the conqueror of Austria. General Hartmann said, "Having passed my life on battle-fields, I have often seen death, but I never saw a soldier die more bravely."

When near death, Napoleon II. said, "So young, and is there no remedy? My birth and my death will be the only points of remembrance." He lies buried in the plain Church of the Capucines, beside his mother. His heart is in a small silver urn in St. Augustine's Church.

For six years Napoleon lived in this prison at St. Helena, dictating his memoirs and commentaries to Count Montholon, Baron Gourgaud, and Count Las Cases. His health failed rapidly after the first year. Not taking exercise, on account of the constant espionage, he was finally prevailed upon by the physician to work a little in a garden, which he found a relief.

At the end of a year, Las Cases was banished with his son to

England, because he had forwarded a letter to Lady Clavering, telling how badly the Emperor was treated, and it had not passed through the hands of Sir Hudson Lowe. This was a great blow to Napoleon, as he was the only one who could read, speak, and understand English. Dr. O'Meara was also obliged to leave St. Helena on account of Sir Hudson Lowe's treatment of him.

After some months of illness, the friends of Napoleon were permitted to send Dr. Antommarchi, a Corsican, to him. In the spring of 1821, Napoleon grew feeble and emaciated. He made his will, remembering his friends most generously. April 22, from perspiration on account of his great pain, Count Montholon writes, "On this night I changed the Emperor's linen seven times." April 25, as Montholon watched by his bedside, at four o'clock in the morning, Napoleon exclaimed, "I have just seen my good Josephine, but she would not embrace me. She disappeared at the moment when I was about to take her in my arms. She was seated there . . . She is not changed. She is still the same, full of devotion to me. She told me that we were about to see each other again, never more to part. Did you see her?"

Three days later he gave directions about his death, asking that his heart might be put in spirits of wine, and carried to Parma, to Marie Louise. "You will tell her that I tenderly loved her," he said, "that I never ceased to love her."

Five days before his death he dictated for two hours his desires about the Palace of Versailles, and the organization of the National Guard for the defence of Paris. To the last he carried out his chosen motto, "Everything for the French people."

He remembered his servants, and wished to see them and say good-by. One of them exclaimed excitedly, "I will die for him."

May 2 the Emperor was delirious, and, thinking he was with his army, shouted, "Desaix! Massena! Ah! victory is declaring. Run! hasten! press the charge! They are ours!" He sprang from the bed and fell prostrate upon the floor.

On the night of May 4 a tornado swept the island, uprooting the trees which the Emperor had planted. During the night, says Count Montholon, "Twice I thought I distinguished the unconnected words, *'France—armée, tête d'armée* (head of the army)—Josephine.'"

During the whole of May 5 he lay quiet and peaceful, conscious, his right hand out of bed, seemingly absorbed in deep meditation. At eleven minutes before six o'clock he died.

England would not permit his body to be embalmed or to be carried to France, as he had requested, or his heart to be given to Marie Louise; so, at half-past twelve, on May 8, he was buried under some willows at St. Helena. The English garrison, two thousand five hundred strong, which had been on the island to keep Napoleon from escaping, now followed his body to the grave. Three volleys of fifteen guns each were fired over it. The soldiers had unbounded admiration for the unrivalled leader, and begged to kiss the blue cloak which he wore at Marengo, and which was thrown over the coffin.

"We were not allowed," says Dr. Antommarchi, "to place over the grave either a stone or a modest inscription, the governor [Sir Hudson Lowe] opposing this pious wish."

The Emperor had written in his will, "It is my wish that my ashes may repose on the banks of the Seine, in the midst of the French people, whom I have loved so well."

On May 5, 1840, nineteen years after Napoleon's death, the French, now that Louis Philippe had become king, asked England that his body might be removed to France. Consent being given, Prince de Joinville, the son of the king, with Gourgaud, Bertrand, and the son of Las Cases, with two armed ships, proceeded on their sad errand, bearing an ebony coffin, with the one word, "Napoleon," on it in gold letters. Within was a coffin of lead. The funeral pall was of purple velvet, embroidered with bees, and bordered with ermine.

At midnight, Oct. 5, 1840, the work of exhuming the body of the Emperor was begun. At ten o'clock in the forenoon the coffin was reached, so difficult had it been to remove the heavy stones and cement which covered the vault. The first coffin of mahogany was opened, then the leaden one, then one of mahogany, then one of tin. The body was found wonderfully preserved, and seemed as though recently interred. The hands were perfect, with the smooth skin as if in life. The clothes retained their color,—the dark green coat faced with red, the white pantaloons, and the hat, resting on the thigh. The body was exposed to the air only two minutes; the coffins were re-sealed and placed in those brought from France.

The ships reached France early in December. Never was there such a funeral in Paris. One hundred and fifty thousand soldiers and more than a million citizens assisted at the magnificent obsequies. The funeral car, its cenotaph rising fifty feet from the ground, was drawn by sixteen black horses, four abreast, covered with cloth of gold. The Emperor's war-horse was draped with a veil of purple crape, embroidered with bees. The remnants of the Old Guard were there—the hosts who idolized Napoleon and would have died for him; but the son, the King of Rome, was sleeping in a coffin in Austria, and Josephine was resting in the church at Rueil, two miles from Malmaison.

At the funeral service three hundred musicians played Mozart's Requiem in the Church of the Invalides, where now the great hero rests. The seemingly countless throng of people were moved to tears. Could he who was its object have looked forward to all this love and homage, when he lay dying among the rocks of St. Helena, the agony might have been lessened. Could he have foreseen how tens of thousands, every year, from all the world, would stand by that tomb, under the dome of the Invalides, and do honor to the wonderful soldier and statesman, that bitter exile and death might not have been quite so desolate and pathetic.

"Posterity," as he said, "will do him justice." Already the harshness of his critics is giving place to a correct estimate of his extraordinary genius.

"I have formed and carried into effect," he said to Dr. O'Meara, "a code of laws that will bear my name to the most

147

distant posterity. From nothing I raised myself to be the most powerful monarch of the world."

Napier thought Napoleon "the greatest man of whom history makes mention." "Never," says Alison, "were talents of the highest, genius of the most exalted kind, more profusely bestowed upon a human being."

Napoleon worked incessantly. He saved every moment. He believed in himself. He had great courage, will, and energy. He said to Las Cases that he liked *two-o'clock-in-the-morning courage*, which he had rarely met. "I mean," he said, "unprepared courage; that which is necessary on an unexpected occasion, and which, in spite of the most unforeseen events, leaves full freedom of judgment and decision."

Napoleon had this courage. Three horses were killed under him at Toulon, several in Italy, and three or four at the siege of Saint Jean d'Acre. When his body was prepared for burial, it was found that there were several scars upon it, some slight, and three very distinct.

He hated selfishness. Madame la Générale Durant, first lady to the Empress Marie Louise, relates in her book, "Napoleon and Marie Louise," that once, when Marie Louise said everybody was selfish, and that she was also, he replied, "Don't say, my Louise, that you are selfish; I know no more hideous vice."

He had great dignity combined with kindliness. After a ball, during which he conversed with Goethe, he wrote Josephine: "I have attended a ball in Weimar. The Emperor Alexander danced. But I? No! Forty years are forty years."

"He had a directness of action," says Emerson, "never before combined with so much comprehension . . . Here was a man who, in each moment and emergency, knew what to do next . . . Few men have any next; they live from hand to mouth, without plan, and are ever at the end of their line, and, after each action, wait for an impulse from abroad. Napoleon had been the first man of the world, if his ends had been purely public . . .

"We cannot, in the universal imbecility, indecision, and

148

indolence of men, sufficiently congratulate ourselves on this strong and ready actor, who took occasion by the beard, and showed us how much may be accomplished by the mere force of such virtues as all men possess in less degrees; namely, by punctuality, by personal attention, by courage and thoroughness."

While indomitable in battle, he was, says General Gourgaud, "of all generals, whether ancient or modern, the one who has paid the greatest attention to the wounded. The intoxication of victory never could make him forget them. His first thought after every battle was always of them."

Count Segur relates that, after the battle of Borodino, when Napoleon and his escort were going over the field, a horse stepped on a dying man, who expired with a groan. Napoleon uttered a shriek of pain. Some one, to soothe him, said, "It was only a Russian." With much warmth, Napoleon replied, "After victory there are no enemies, but only men."

His despatch was marvellous. He was generous, and never forgot the poorest who needed his kindness. He was ambitious; but Europe, fearing him, forced him into many of his wars. He knew how to govern himself as well as others. He said of Lannes, one of his generals who lost his temper, that a man could not be great who permitted himself to get angry. The officer heard of this remark, and ever after controlled his temper.

Napoleon was more moral than his age. He loved children and nature. "How many times," says Bourrienne, as they walked toward Rueil from Malmaison, "has the bell of the village church interrupted our most serious conversations! He would stop, lest the noise of our footsteps should drown any portion of the delightful sound."

He believed, in an age of unbelief. He said to Bertrand at St. Helena, "I know men, and I tell you that Jesus Christ is not a man . . . Everything in him astonishes me. His spirit overawes me, and his will confounds me. Between him and whoever else in the world there is no possible term of comparison."

Napoleon compared the reign of Christ with that of Cæsar, Alexander, Hannibal, and of himself; "My armies have forgotten me, even while living, as the Carthaginian army forgot Hannibal. Such is our power! A single battle lost crushes us, and adversity scatters our friends . . . What an abyss between my deep misery and the eternal reign of Christ, which is proclaimed, loved, adored, and which is extended over all the earth! Is this to die? Is it not rather to live? The death of Christ! It is the death of God."

The life of Napoleon, truly called "the Great," is more interesting and pathetic than any novel. It will always remain one of the marvels of the world.

A CHAPTER FROM
Famous Leaders Among Men, 1894

NAPOLEON AND MARIE WALEWSKA

By Lyndon Orr

There are four women who may be said to have deeply influenced the life of Napoleon. These four are the only ones who need to be taken into account by the student of his imperial career. The great emperor was susceptible to feminine charms at all times; but just as it used to be said of him that "his smile never rose above his eyes," so it might as truly be said that in most instances the throbbing of his heart did not affect his actions.

Women to him were the creatures of the moment, although he might seem to care for them and to show his affection in extravagant ways, as in his affair with Mlle. Georges, the beautiful but rather tiresome actress. As for Mme. de Stael, she bored him to distraction by her assumption of wisdom. That was not the kind of woman that Napoleon cared for. He preferred that a woman should be womanly, and not a sort of owl to sit and talk with him about the theory of government.

When it came to married women they interested him only because of the children they might bear to grow up as recruits for his insatiate armies. At the public balls given at the Tuileries he would walk about the gorgeous drawing-rooms, and when a lady was presented to him he would snap out, sharply:

"How many children have you?"

If she were able to answer that she had several the emperor would look pleased and would pay her some compliment; but if she said that she had none he would turn upon her sharply and say:

"Then go home and have some!"

Of the four women who influenced his life, first must come Josephine, because she secured him his earliest chance of advancement. She met him through Barras, with whom she was said to be rather intimate. The young soldier was fascinated by her—the more because she was older than he and possessed all the practised arts of the creole and the woman of the world. When she married him she brought him as her dowry the command of the army of Italy, where in a few months he made the tri-color, borne by ragged troops, triumphant over the splendidly equipped hosts of Austria.

She was his first love, and his knowledge of her perfidy gave him the greatest shock and horror of his whole life; yet she might have held him to the end if she had borne an heir to the imperial throne. It was her failure to do so that led Napoleon to divorce Josephine and marry the thick-lipped Marie Louise of Austria. There were times later when he showed signs of regret and said:

"I have had no luck since I gave up Josephine!"

Marie Louise was of importance for a time—the short time when she entertained her husband and delighted him by giving birth to the little King of Rome. Yet in the end she was but an episode; fleeing from her husband in his misfortune, becoming the mistress of Count Neipperg, and letting her son—l'Aiglon—die in a land that was far from France.

Napoleon's sister, Pauline Bonaparte, was the third woman who comes to mind when we contemplate the great Corsican's career. She, too, is an episode. During the period of his ascendancy she plagued him with her wanton ways, her sauciness and trickery. It was amusing to throw him into one of his violent rages; but Pauline was true at heart, and when her great brother was sent to Elba she followed him devotedly and gave him all her store of jewels, including the famous Borghese diamonds, perhaps the most superb of all gems known to the western world. She would gladly have followed him, also, to St. Helena had she been permitted. Remaining behind, she did everything possible in conspiring to secure his freedom.

But, after all, Pauline and Marie Louise count for comparatively little. Josephine's fate was interwoven with Napoleon's; and, with his Corsican superstition, he often said so. The fourth woman, of whom I am writing here, may be said to have almost equaled Josephine in her influence on the emperor as well as in the pathos of her life-story.

On New-Year's Day of 1807 Napoleon, who was then almost Emperor of Europe, passed through the little town of Bronia, in Poland. Riding with his cavalry to Warsaw, the ancient capital of the Polish kingdom, he seemed a very demigod of battle.

True, he had had to abandon his long-cherished design of invading and overrunning England, and Nelson had shattered his fleets and practically driven his flag from the sea; but the naval disaster of Trafalgar had speedily been followed by the triumph of Austerlitz, the greatest and most brilliant of all Napoleon's victories, which left Austria and Russia humbled to the very ground before him.

Then Prussia had dared to defy the over-bearing conqueror and had put into the field against him her armies trained by Frederick the Great; but these he had shattered almost at a stroke, winning in one day the decisive battles of Jena and Auerstadt. He had stabled his horses in the royal palace of the Hohenzollerns and had pursued the remnant of the Prussian forces to the Russian border.

As he marched into the Polish provinces the people swarmed by thousands to meet him and hail him as their country's savior. They believed down to the very last that Bonaparte would make the Poles once more a free and independent nation and rescue them from the tyranny of Russia.

Napoleon played upon this feeling in every manner known to his artful mind. He used it to alarm the Czar. He used it to intimidate the Emperor of Austria; but more especially did he use it among the Poles themselves to win for his armies thousands upon thousands of gallant soldiers, who believed that in fighting for Napoleon they were fighting for the final independence of their native land.

Therefore, with the intensity of patriotism which is a passion among the Poles, every man and every woman gazed at Napoleon with something like adoration; for was not he the mighty warrior who had in his gift what all desired? Soldiers of every rank swarmed to his standards. Princes and nobles flocked about him. Those who stayed at home repeated wonderful stories of his victories and prayed for him and fed the flame which spread through all the country. It was felt that no sacrifice was too great to win his favor; that to him, as to a deity, everything that he desired should be yielded up, since he was to restore the liberty of Poland.

And hence, when the carriage of the emperor dashed into Bronia, surrounded by Polish lancers and French cuirassiers, the enormous crowd surged forward and blocked the way so that their hero could not pass because of their cheers and cries and supplications.

In the midst of it all there came a voice of peculiar sweetness from the thickest portion of the crowd.

"Please let me pass!" said the voice. "Let me see him, if only for a moment!"

The populace rolled backward, and through the lane which they made a beautiful girl with dark blue eyes that flamed and streaming hair that had become loosened about her radiant face was confronting the emperor. Carried away by her enthusiasm, she cried:

"Thrice welcome to Poland! We can do or say nothing to express our joy in the country which you will surely deliver from its tyrant."

The emperor bowed and, with a smile, handed a great bouquet of roses to the girl, for her beauty and her enthusiasm had made a deep impression on him.

"Take it," said he, "as a proof of my admiration. I trust that I may have the pleasure of meeting you at Warsaw and of hearing your thanks from those beautiful lips."

In a moment more the trumpets rang out shrilly, the horsemen closed up beside the imperial carriage, and it rolled away amid the tumultuous shouting of the populace.

The girl who had so attracted Napoleon's attention was Marie Walewska, descended from an ancient though impoverished family in Poland. When she was only fifteen she was courted by one of the wealthiest men in Poland, the Count Walewska. He was three or four times her age, yet her dark blue eyes, her massive golden hair, and the exquisite grace of her figure led him to plead that she might become his wife. She had accepted him, but the marriage was that of a mere child, and her interest still centered upon her country and took the form of patriotism rather than that of wifehood and maternity.

It was for this reason that the young Countess had visited Bronia. She was now eighteen years of age and still had the sort of romantic feeling which led her to think that she would keep in some secret hiding-place the bouquet which the greatest man alive had given her.

But Napoleon was not the sort of man to forget anything that had given him either pleasure or the reverse. He who, at the height of his cares, could recall instantly how many cannon were in each seaport of France and could make out an accurate list of all his military stores; he who could call by name every soldier in his guard, with a full remembrance of the battles each man had fought in and the honors that he had won—he was not likely to forget so lovely a face as the one which had gleamed with peculiar radiance through the crowd at Bronia.

On reaching Warsaw he asked one or two well-informed persons about this beautiful stranger. Only a few hours had passed before Prince Poniatowski, accompanied by other nobles, called upon her at her home.

"I am directed, madam," said he, "by order of the Emperor of France, to bid you to be present at a ball that is to be given in his honor to-morrow evening."

Mme. Walewska was startled, and her face grew hot with blushes. Did the emperor remember her escapade at Bronia? If so, how had he discovered her? Why should he seek her out and do her such an honor?

"That, madam, is his imperial majesty's affair," Poniatowski told her. "I merely obey his instructions and ask your presence at the ball. Perhaps Heaven has marked you out to be the means of saving our unhappy country."

In this way, by playing on her patriotism, Poniatowski almost persuaded her, and yet something held her back. She trembled, though she was greatly fascinated; and finally she refused to go.

Scarcely had the envoy left her, however, when a great company of nobles entered in groups and begged her to humor the emperor. Finally her own husband joined in their entreaties and actually commanded her to go; so at last she was compelled to yield.

It was by no means the frank and radiant girl who was now preparing again to meet the emperor. She knew not why, and yet her heart was full of trepidation and nervous fright, the cause of which she could not guess, yet which made her task a severe ordeal. She dressed herself in white satin, with no adornment save a wreath of foliage in her hair.

As she entered the ballroom she was welcomed by hundreds whom she had never seen before, but who were of the highest nobility of Poland. Murmurs of admiration followed her, and finally Poniatowski came to her and complimented her, besides bringing her a message that the emperor desired her to dance with him.

"I am very sorry," she said, with a quiver of the lips, "but I really cannot dance. Be kind enough to ask the emperor to excuse me."

But at that very moment she felt some strange magnetic influence; and without looking up she could feel that Napoleon himself was standing by her as she sat with blanched face and downcast eyes, not daring to look up at him.

"White upon white is a mistake, madam," said the emperor, in his gentlest tones. Then, stooping low, he whispered, "I had expected a far different reception."

She neither smiled nor met his eyes. He stood there for a moment and then passed on, leaving her to return to her home with a heavy heart. The young countess felt that she had acted wrongly, and yet there was an instinct—an instinct that she could not conquer.

In the gray of the morning, while she was still tossing feverishly, her maid knocked at the door and brought her a hastily scribbled note. It ran as follows:

I saw none but you, I admired none but you; I desire only you. Answer at once, and calm the impatient ardor of—N.

These passionate words burned from her eyes the veil that had hidden the truth from her. What before had been mere blind instinct became an actual verity. Why had she at first rushed forth into the very streets to hail the possible deliverer of her country, and then why had she shrunk from him when he sought to honor her! It was all clear enough now. This bedside missive meant that he had intended her dishonor and that he had looked upon her simply as a possible mistress.

At once she crushed the note angrily in her hand.

"There is no answer at all," said she, bursting into bitter tears at the very thought that he should dare to treat her in this way.

But on the following morning when she awoke her maid was standing beside her with a second letter from Napoleon. She refused to open it and placed it in a packet with the first letter, and ordered that both of them should be returned to the emperor.

She shrank from speaking to her husband of what had happened, and there was no one else in whom she dared confide. All through that day there came hundreds of visitors, either of princely rank or men who had won fame by their gallantry and courage. They all begged to see her, but to them all she sent one answer—that she was ill and could see no one.

After a time her husband burst into her room, and insisted that she should see them.

"Why," exclaimed he, "you are insulting the greatest men and the noblest women of Poland! More than that, there are some of the most distinguished Frenchmen sitting at your doorstep, as it were. There is Duroc, grand marshal of France, and in refusing to see him you are insulting the great emperor on whom depends everything that our country longs for. Napoleon has invited you to a state dinner and you have given him no answer whatever. I order you to rise at once and receive these ladies and gentlemen who have done you so much honor!"

She could not refuse. Presently she appeared in her drawing-room, where she was at once surrounded by an immense throng of her own countrymen and countrywomen, who made no pretense of misunderstanding the situation. To them, what was one woman's honor when compared with the freedom and independence of their nation? She was overwhelmed by arguments and entreaties. She was even accused of being disloyal to the cause of Poland if she refused her consent.

One of the strangest documents of that period was a letter sent to her and signed by the noblest men in Poland. It contained a powerful appeal to her patriotism. One remarkable passage even quotes the Bible to point out her line of duty. A portion of this letter ran as follows:

Did Esther, think you, give herself to Ahasuerus out of the fulness of her love for him? So great was the terror with which he inspired her that she fainted at the sight of him. We may therefore conclude that affection had but little to do with her resolve. She sacrificed her own inclinations to the salvation of her country, and that salvation it was her glory to achieve. May we be enabled to say the same of you, to your glory and our own happiness!

After this letter came others from Napoleon himself, full of the most humble pleading. It was not wholly distasteful thus to have the conqueror of the world seek her out and offer her his adoration any more than it was distasteful to think that the revival of her own nation depended on her single will. M. Frederic Masson, whose minute studies regarding everything relating to Napoleon have won him a seat in the French Academy, writes of Marie Walewska at this time: Every force was now brought into play against her. Her country, her friends, her religion, the Old and the New Testaments, all urged her to yield; they all combined for the ruin of a simple and inexperienced girl of eighteen who had no parents, whose husband even thrust her into temptation, and whose friends thought that her downfall would be her glory.

Amid all these powerful influences she consented to attend the dinner. To her gratification Napoleon treated her with distant courtesy, and, in fact, with a certain coldness.

"I heard that Mme. Walewska was indisposed. I trust that she has recovered," was all the greeting that he gave her when they met.

Every one else with whom she spoke overwhelmed her with flattery and with continued urging; but the emperor himself for a time acted as if she had displeased him. This was consummate art; for as soon as she was relieved of her fears she began to regret that she had thrown her power away.

During the dinner she let her eyes wander to those of the emperor almost in supplication. He, the subtlest of men, knew that he had won. His marvelous eyes met hers and drew her attention to him as by an electric current; and when the ladies left the great dining-room Napoleon sought her out and whispered in her ear a few words of ardent love.

It was too little to alarm her seriously now. It was enough to make her feel that magnetism which Napoleon knew so well how to evoke and exercise. Again every one crowded about her with congratulations. Some said:

"He never even saw any of US. His eyes were all for YOU! They flashed fire as he looked at you."

"You have conquered his heart," others said, "and you can

do what you like with him. The salvation of Poland is in your hands."

The company broke up at an early hour, but Mme. Walewska was asked to remain. When she was alone General Duroc—one of the emperor's favorite officers and most trusted lieutenants— entered and placed a letter from Napoleon in her lap. He tried to tell her as tactfully as possible how much harm she was doing by refusing the imperial request. She was deeply affected, and presently, when Duroc left her, she opened the letter which he had given her and read it. It was worded thus:

> There are times when all splendors become oppressive, as I feel but too deeply at the present moment. How can I satisfy the desires of a heart that yearns to cast itself at your feet, when its impulses are checked at every point by considerations of the highest moment? Oh, if you would, you alone might overcome the obstacles that keep us apart. MY FRIEND DUROC WILL MAKE ALL EASY FOR YOU. Oh, come, come! Your every wish shall be gratified! Your country will be dearer to me when you take pity on my poor heart. N.

Every chance of escape seemed to be closed. She had Napoleon's own word that he would free Poland in return for her self-sacrifice. Moreover, her powers of resistance had been so weakened that, like many women, she temporized. She decided that she would meet the emperor alone. She would tell him that she did not love him, and yet would plead with him to save her beloved country.

As she sat there every tick of the clock stirred her to a new excitement. At last there came a knock upon the door, a cloak was thrown about her from behind, a heavy veil was drooped about her golden hair, and she was led, by whom she knew not, to the street, where a finely appointed carriage was waiting for her. No sooner had she entered it than she was driven rapidly through the darkness to the beautifully carved entrance of a palace. Half led, half carried, she was taken up the steps to a door which was eagerly opened by some one within. There were warmth and light and color and the scent of flowers as she was placed in a comfortable arm-chair. Her wrappings were taken from her, the door was closed behind her; and then, as she looked up, she found herself in the presence of Napoleon, who was kneeling at her feet and uttering soothing words.

Wisely, the emperor used no violence. He merely argued with her; he told her over and over his love for her; and finally he declared that for her sake he would make Poland once again a strong and splendid kingdom.

Several hours passed. In the early morning, before daylight, there came a knock at the door.

"Already?" said Napoleon. "Well, my plaintive dove, go home and rest. You must not fear the eagle. In time you will come to love him, and in all things you shall command him."

Then he led her to the door, but said that he would not open it unless she promised to see him the next day—a promise which she gave the more readily because he had treated her with such respect.

On the following morning her faithful maid came to her bedside with a cluster of beautiful violets, a letter, and several daintily made morocco cases. When these were opened there leaped out strings and necklaces of exquisite diamonds, blazing in the morning sunlight. Mme. Walewska seized the jewels and flung them across the room with an order that they should be taken back at once to the imperial giver; but the letter, which was in the same romantic strain as the others, she retained.

On that same evening there was another dinner, given to the emperor by the nobles, and Marie Walewska attended it, but of course without the diamonds, which she had returned. Nor did she wear the flowers which had accompanied the diamonds.

When Napoleon met her he frowned upon her and made her tremble with the cold glances that shot from his eyes of steel.

He scarcely spoke to her throughout the meal, but those who sat beside her were earnest in their pleading.

Again she waited until the guests had gone away, and with a lighter heart, since she felt that she had nothing to fear. But when she met Napoleon in his private cabinet, alone, his mood was very different from that which he had shown before. Instead of gentleness and consideration he was the Napoleon of camps, and not of courts. He greeted her bruskly.

"I scarcely expected to see you again," said he. "Why did you refuse my diamonds and my flowers? Why did you avoid my eyes at dinner? Your coldness is an insult which I shall not brook." Then he raised his voice to that rasping, almost blood-curdling tone which even his hardiest soldiers dreaded: "I will have you know that I mean to conquer you. You SHALL—yes, I repeat it, you SHALL love me! I have restored the name of your country. It owes its very existence to me."

Then he resorted to a trick which he had played years before in dealing with the Austrians at Campo Formio.

"See this watch which I am holding in my hand. Just as I dash it to fragments before you, so will I shatter Poland if you drive me to desperation by rejecting my heart and refusing me your own."

As he spoke he hurled the watch against the opposite wall with terrific force, dashing it to pieces. In terror, Mme. Walewska fainted. When she resumed consciousness there was Napoleon wiping away her tears with the tenderness of a woman and with words of self-reproach.

The long siege was over. Napoleon had conquered, and this girl of eighteen gave herself up to his caresses and endearments, thinking that, after all, her love of country was more than her own honor.

Her husband, as a matter of form, put her away from him, though at heart he approved what she had done, while the Polish people regarded her as nothing less than a national heroine. To them she was no minister to the vices of an emperor, but rather one who would make him love Poland for her sake and restore its greatness.

So far as concerned his love for her, it was, indeed, almost idolatry. He honored her in every way and spent all the time at his disposal in her company. But his promise to restore Poland he never kept, and gradually she found that he had never meant to keep it.

"I love your country," he would say, "and I am willing to aid in the attempt to uphold its rights, but my first duty is to France. I cannot shed French blood in a foreign cause."

By this time, however, Marie Walewska had learned to love Napoleon for his own sake. She could not resist his ardor, which matched the ardor of the Poles themselves. Moreover, it flattered her to see the greatest soldier in the world a suppliant for her smiles.

For some years she was Napoleon's close companion, spending long hours with him and finally accompanying him to Paris. She was the mother of Napoleon's only son who lived to manhood. This son, who bore the name of Alexandre Florian de Walewski, was born in Poland in 1810, and later was created a count and duke of the second French Empire. It may be said parenthetically that he was a man of great ability. Living down to 1868, he was made much of by Napoleon III., who placed him in high offices of state, which he filled with distinction. In contrast with the Duc de Morny, who was Napoleon's illegitimate half-brother, Alexandre de Walewski stood out in brilliant contrast. He would have nothing to do with stock-jobbing and unseemly speculation.

"I may be poor," he said—though he was not poor—"but at least I remember the glory of my father and what is due to his great name."

As for Mme. Walewska, she was loyal to the emperor, and lacked the greed of many women whom he had made his favorites. Even at Elba, when he was in exile and disgrace, she visited him that she might endeavor to console him. She was his counselor and friend as well as his earnestly loved mate. When she died in Paris in 1817, while the dethroned emperor was a prisoner at St. Helena, the word "Napoleon" was the last upon her lips.

A Chapter from
Famous Affinities of History,
VII, *The Romance of Devotion,* 1912

THE STORY OF
PAULINE BONAPARTE

By Lyndon Orr

It was said of Napoleon long ago that he could govern emperors and kings, but that not even he could rule his relatives. He himself once declared:

"My family have done me far more harm than I have been able to do them good."

It would be an interesting historical study to determine just how far the great soldier's family aided in his downfall by their selfishness, their jealousy, their meanness, and their ingratitude.

There is something piquant in thinking of Napoleon as a domestic sort of person. Indeed, it is rather difficult to do so. When we speak his name we think of the stern warrior hurling his armies up bloody slopes and on to bloody victory. He is the man whose steely eyes made his haughtiest marshals tremble, or else the wise, far-seeing statesman and lawgiver; but decidedly he is not a household model. We read of his sharp speech to women, of his outrageous manners at the dinner-table, and of the thousand and one details which Mme. de Remusat has chronicled—and perhaps in part invented, for there has always existed the suspicion that her animus was that of a woman who had herself sought the imperial favor and had failed to win it.

But, in fact, all these stories relate to the Napoleon of courts and palaces, and not to the Napoleon of home. In his private life this great man was not merely affectionate and indulgent, but he even showed a certain weakness where his relatives were concerned, so that he let them prey upon him almost without end.

He had a great deal of the Italian largeness and lavishness of character with his family. When a petty officer he nearly starved himself in order to give his younger brother, Louis, a military education. He was devotedly fond of children, and they were fond of him, as many anecdotes attest. His passionate love for Josephine before he learned of her infidelity is almost painful to read of; and even afterward, when he had been disillusioned, and when she was paying Fouche a thousand francs a day to spy upon Napoleon's every action, he still treated her with friendliness and allowed her extravagance to embarrass him.

He made his eldest brother, Joseph, King of Spain, and Spain proved almost as deadly to him as did Russia. He made his youngest brother, Jerome, King of Westphalia, and Jerome turned the palace into a pigsty and brought discredit on the very name of Bonaparte. His brother Louis, for whom he had starved himself, he placed upon the throne of Holland, and Louis promptly devoted himself to his own interests, conniving at many things which were inimical to France. He was planning high advancement for his brother Lucien, and Lucien suddenly married a disreputable actress and fled with her to England, where he was received with pleasure by the most persistent of all Napoleon's enemies.

So much for his brothers—incompetent, ungrateful, or openly his foes. But his three sisters were no less remarkable in the relations which they bore to him. They have been styled "the three crowned courtesans," and they have been condemned together as being utterly void of principle and monsters of ingratitude.

Much of this censure was well deserved by all of them—by Caroline and Elise and Pauline. But when we look at the facts impartially we shall find something which makes Pauline stand out alone as infinitely superior to her sisters. Of all the Bonapartes she was the only one who showed fidelity and gratitude to the great emperor, her brother. Even Mme. Mere, Napoleon's mother, who beyond all question transmitted to him his great mental and physical power, did nothing for him. At the height of his splendor she hoarded sous and francs and grumblingly remarked:

"All this is for a time. It isn't going to last!"

Pauline, however, was in one respect different from all her kindred. Napoleon made Elise a princess in her own right and gave her the Grand Duchy of Tuscany. He married Caroline to Marshal Murat, and they became respectively King and Queen of Naples. For Pauline he did very little—less, in fact, than for any other member of his family—and yet she alone stood by him to the end.

This feather-headed, languishing, beautiful, distracting morsel of frivolity, who had the manners of a kitten and the morals of a cat, nevertheless was not wholly unworthy to be Napoleon's sister. One has to tell many hard things of her; and yet one almost pardons her because of her underlying devotion to the man who made the name of Bonaparte illustrious for ever. Caroline, Queen of Naples, urged her husband to turn against his former chief. Elise, sour and greedy, threw in her fortunes with the Murats. Pauline, as we shall see, had the one redeeming trait of gratitude.

To those who knew her she was from girlhood an incarnation of what used to be called "femininity." We have to-day another and a higher definition of womanhood, but to her contemporaries, and to many modern writers, she has seemed to be first of all woman—"woman to the tips of her rosy finger-nails," says Levy. Those who saw her were distracted by her loveliness. They say that no one can form any idea of her beauty from her pictures. "A veritable masterpiece of creation," she had been called.

Frederic Masson declares:

She was so much more the typical woman that with her the defects common to women reached their highest development, while her beauty attained a perfection which may justly be called unique.

No one speaks of Pauline Bonaparte's character or of her intellect, but wholly of her loveliness and charm, and, it must be added, of her utter lack of anything like a moral sense.

Even as a child of thirteen, when the Bonapartes left Corsica and took up their abode in Marseilles, she attracted universal attention by her wonderful eyes, her grace, and also by the utter lack of decorum which she showed. The Bonaparte girls at this time lived almost on charity. The future emperor was then a captain of artillery and could give them but little out of his scanty pay.

Pauline—or, as they called her in those days, Paulette—wore unbecoming hats and shabby gowns, and shoes that were full of holes. None the less, she was sought out by several men of note, among them Freron, a commissioner of the Convention. He visited Pauline so often as to cause unfavorable comment; but he was in love with her, and she fell in love with him to the extent of her capacity. She used to write him love letters in Italian, which were certainly not lacking in ardor. Here is the end of one of them:

I love you always and most passionately. I love you for ever, my beautiful idol, my heart, my appealing lover. I love you, love you, love you, the most loved of lovers, and I swear never to love any one else!

This was interesting in view of the fact that soon afterward she fell in love with Junot, who became a famous marshal. But her love affairs never gave her any serious trouble; and the three sisters, who now began to feel the influence of Napoleon's rise to power, enjoyed themselves as they had never done before. At Antibes they had a beautiful villa, and later a mansion at Milan.

By this time Napoleon had routed the Austrians in Italy, and all France was ringing with his name. What was Pauline like in her maidenhood? Arnault says:

She was an extraordinary combination of perfect physical

beauty and the strangest moral laxity. She was as pretty as you please, but utterly unreasonable. She had no more manners than a school-girl—talking incoherently, giggling at everything and nothing, and mimicking the most serious persons of rank.

General de Ricard, who knew her then, tells in his monograph of the private theatricals in which Pauline took part, and of the sport which they had behind the scenes. He says:

The Bonaparte girls used literally to dress us. They pulled our ears and slapped us, but they always kissed and made up later. We used to stay in the girls' room all the time when they were dressing.

Napoleon was anxious to see his sisters in some way settled. He proposed to General Marmont to marry Pauline. The girl was then only seventeen, and one might have had some faith in her character. But Marmont was shrewd and knew her far too well. The words in which he declined the honor are interesting:

"I know that she is charming and exquisitely beautiful; yet I have dreams of domestic happiness, of fidelity, and of virtue. Such dreams are seldom realized, I know. Still, in the hope of winning them—"

And then he paused, coughed, and completed what he had to say in a sort of mumble, but his meaning was wholly clear. He would not accept the offer of Pauline in marriage, even though she was the sister of his mighty chief.

Then Napoleon turned to General Leclerc, with whom Pauline had for some time flirted, as she had flirted with almost all the officers of Napoleon's staff. Leclerc was only twenty-six. He was rich and of good manners, but rather serious and in poor health. This was not precisely the sort of husband for Pauline, if we look at it in the conventional way; but it served Napoleon's purpose and did not in the least interfere with his sister's intrigues.

Poor Leclerc, who really loved Pauline, grew thin, and graver still in manner. He was sent to Spain and Portugal, and finally was made commander-in-chief of the French expedition to

Haiti, where the famous black rebel, Toussaint l'Ouverture, was heading an uprising of the negroes. Napoleon ordered Pauline to accompany her husband. Pauline flatly refused, although she made this an occasion for ordering "mountains of pretty clothes and pyramids of hats." But still she refused to go on board the flag-ship. Leclerc expostulated and pleaded, but the lovely witch laughed in his face and still persisted that she would never go.

Word was brought to Napoleon. He made short work of her resistance.

"Bring a litter," he said, with one of his steely glances. "Order six grenadiers to thrust her into it, and see that she goes on board forthwith."

And so, screeching like an angry cat, she was carried on board, and set sail with her husband and one of her former lovers. She found Haiti and Santo Domingo more agreeable than she had supposed. She was there a sort of queen who could do as she pleased and have her orders implicitly obeyed. Her dissipation was something frightful. Her folly and her vanity were beyond belief.

But at the end of two years both she and her husband fell ill. He was stricken down by the yellow fever, which was decimating the French army. Pauline was suffering from the results of her life in a tropical climate. Leclerc died, the expedition was abandoned, and Pauline brought the general's body back to France. When he was buried she, still recovering from her fever, had him interred in a costly coffin and paid him the tribute of cutting off her beautiful hair and burying it with him.

"What a touching tribute to her dead husband!" said some one to Napoleon.

The emperor smiled cynically as he remarked:

"H'm! Of course she knows that her hair is bound to fall out after her fever, and that it will come in longer and thicker for being cropped."

Napoleon, in fact, though he loved Pauline better than his other sisters—or perhaps because he loved her better—was very strict with her. He obliged her to wear mourning, and to observe some of the proprieties; but it was hard to keep her within bounds.

Presently it became noised about that Prince Camillo Borghese was exceedingly intimate with her. The prince was an excellent specimen of the fashionable Italian. He was immensely rich. His palace at Rome was crammed with pictures, statues, and every sort of artistic treasure. He was the owner, moreover, of the famous Borghese jewels, the finest collection of diamonds in the world.

Napoleon rather sternly insisted upon her marrying Borghese. Fortunately, the prince was very willing to be connected with Napoleon; while Pauline was delighted at the idea of having diamonds that would eclipse all the gems which Josephine possessed; for, like all of the Bonapartes, she detested her brother's wife. So she would be married and show her diamonds to Josephine. It was a bit of feminine malice which she could not resist.

The marriage took place very quietly at Joseph Bonaparte's house, because of the absence of Napoleon; but the newly made princess was invited to visit Josephine at the palace of Saint-Cloud. Here was to be the triumph of her life. She spent many days in planning a toilet that should be absolutely crushing to Josephine. Whatever she wore must be a background for the famous diamonds. Finally she decided on green velvet.

When the day came Pauline stood before a mirror and gazed at herself with diamonds glistening in her hair, shimmering around her neck, and fastened so thickly on her green velvet gown as to remind one of a moving jewel-casket. She actually shed tears for joy. Then she entered her carriage and drove out to Saint-Cloud.

But the Creole Josephine, though no longer young, was a woman of great subtlety as well as charm. Stories had been told to her of the green velvet, and therefore she had her drawing-room redecorated in the most uncompromising blue. It killed the green velvet completely. As for the diamonds, she met that maneuver by wearing not a single gem of any kind. Her dress was an Indian muslin with a broad hem of gold.

Her exquisite simplicity, coupled with her dignity of bearing, made the Princess Pauline, with her shower of diamonds, and her green velvet displayed against the blue, seem absolutely vulgar. Josephine was most generous in her admiration of the Borghese gems, and she kissed Pauline on parting. The victory was hers.

There is another story of a defeat which Pauline met from another lady, one Mme. de Coutades. This was at a magnificent ball given to the most fashionable world of Paris. Pauline decided upon going, and intended, in her own phrase, to blot out every woman there. She kept the secret of her toilet absolutely, and she entered the ballroom at the psychological moment, when all the guests had just assembled.

She appeared; and at sight of her the music stopped, silence fell upon the assemblage, and a sort of quiver went through every one. Her costume was of the finest muslin bordered with golden palm-leaves. Four bands, spotted like a leopard's skin, were wound about her head, while these in turn were supported by little clusters of golden grapes. She had copied the head-dress of a Bacchante in the Louvre.

All over her person were cameos, and just beneath her breasts she wore a golden band held in place by an engraved gem. Her beautiful wrists, arms, and hands were bare. She had, in fact, blotted out her rivals.

Nevertheless, Mme. de Coutades took her revenge. She went up to Pauline, who was lying on a divan to set off her loveliness, and began gazing at the princess through a double eye-glass. Pauline felt flattered for a moment, and then became uneasy. The lady who was looking at her said to a companion, in a tone of compassion:

"What a pity! She really would be lovely if it weren't for THAT!"

"For what?" returned her escort.

"Why, are you blind? It's so remarkable that you SURELY must see it."

Pauline was beginning to lose her self-composure. She flushed and looked wildly about, wondering what was meant. Then she heard Mme. Coutades say:

"Why, her ears. If I had such ears as those I would cut them off!"

Pauline gave one great gasp and fainted dead away. As a matter of fact, her ears were not so bad. They were simply very flat and colorless, forming a contrast with the rosy tints of her face. But from that moment no one could see anything but these ears; and thereafter the princess wore her hair low enough to cover them.

This may be seen in the statue of her by Canova. It was considered a very daring thing for her to pose for him in the nude, for only a bit of drapery is thrown over her lower limbs. Yet it is true that this statue is absolutely classical in its conception and execution, and its interest is heightened by the fact that its model was what she afterward styled herself, with true Napoleonic pride—"a sister of Bonaparte."

Pauline detested Josephine and was pleased when Napoleon divorced her; but she also disliked the Austrian archduchess, Marie Louise, who was Josephine's successor. On one occasion, at a great court function, she got behind the empress and ran out her tongue at her, in full view of all the nobles and distinguished persons present. Napoleon's eagle eye flashed upon Pauline and blazed like fire upon ice. She actually took to her heels, rushed out of the ball, and never visited the court again.

It would require much time to tell of her other eccentricities, of her intrigues, which were innumerable, of her quarrel with her husband, and of the minor breaches of decorum with which she startled Paris. One of these was her choice of a huge negro to bathe her every morning. When some one ventured to protest, she answered, naively:

"What! Do you call that thing a MAN?"

And she compromised by compelling her black servitor to go out and marry some one at once, so that he might continue his ministrations with propriety!

To her Napoleon showed himself far more severe than with either Caroline or Elise. He gave her a marriage dowry of half a million francs when she became the Princess Borghese, but after that he was continually checking her extravagances. Yet in 1814, when the downfall came and Napoleon was sent into exile at Elba, Pauline was the only one of all his relatives to visit him and spend her time with him. His wife fell away and went back to her Austrian relatives. Of all the Bonapartes only Pauline and Mme. Mere remained faithful to the emperor.

Even then Napoleon refused to pay a bill of hers for sixty-two francs, while he allowed her only two hundred and forty francs for the maintenance of her horses. But she, with a generosity of which one would have thought her quite incapable, gave to her brother a great part of her fortune. When he escaped from Elba and began the campaign of 1815 she presented him with all the Borghese diamonds. In fact, he had them with him in his carriage at Waterloo, where they were captured by the English. Contrast this with the meanness and ingratitude of her sisters and her brothers, and one may well believe that she was sincerely proud of what it meant to be la soeur de Bonaparte.

When he was sent to St. Helena she was ill in bed and could not accompany him. Nevertheless, she tried to sell all her trinkets, of which she was so proud, in order that she might give him help.

When he died she received the news with bitter tears "on hearing all the particulars of that long agony."

As for herself, she did not long survive.

At the age of forty-four her last moments came. Knowing that she was to die, she sent for Prince Borghese and sought a reconciliation. But, after all, she died as she had lived—"the queen of trinkets" (la reine des colifichets).

She asked the servant to bring a mirror. She gazed into it with her dying eyes; and then, as she sank back, it was with a smile of deep content.

"I am not afraid to die," she said. "I am still beautiful!"

A Chapter from
Famous Affinities of History,
VII, *The Romance of Devotion,* 1912

NAPOLEON'S WILL

"Napoleon.

"This 15th April, 1821, at Longwood, Island of St. Helena. This is my Testament or act of my last will.

"1. I die in the Apostolical Roman religion, in the bosom of which I was born, more than fifty years since.

"2. It is my wish that my ashes may repose on the banks of the Seine, in the midst of the French people, whom I have loved so well.

"3. I have always had reason to be pleased with my dearest wife, Maria-Louisa. I retain for her, to my last moment, the most tender sentiments. I beseech her to watch, in order to preserve my son from the snares which yet environ his infancy.

"4. I recommend to my son, never to forget that he was born a French prince, and never to allow himself to become an instrument in the hands of the triumvirs who oppress the nations of Europe; he ought never to fight against France, or injure her in any manner; he ought to adopt my motto: '*Everything for the French people.*'

"5. I die prematurely, assassinated by the English oligarchy and its . . .

"The English nation will not be slow in avenging me.

"6. The two unfortunate results of the invasions of France, when she had still so many resources, are to be attributed to the treason of Marmont, Augereau, Talleyrand, and La Fayette.

"I forgive them—may the posterity of France forgive them as I do.

"7. I thank my good and most excellent mother, the Cardinal, my brothers, Joseph, Lucien, and Jerome, Pauline, Caroline, Julie, Hortense, Catherine, Eugène, for the interest they have continued to feel for me. I pardon Louis for the libel he published in 1820; it is replete with false assertions and falsified documents.

"8. I disavow the *Manuscript of St. Helena*, and other works, under the title of *Maxims*, *Sayings*, etc., which persons have been pleased to publish for the last six years. Such are not the rules which have guided my life. I caused the Duc d'Enghien to be arrested and tried, because that step was essential to the safety, interest, and honor of the French people, when the Comte d'Artois was maintaining, by his own confession, sixty assassins at Paris. Under similar circumstances I should act in the same way."

HISTORIC DOUBTS
RELATIVE TO
NAPOLEON BUONAPARTE

By Richard Whately

Written in 1819, while Napoleon Bonaparte
was still alive, this piece of satire suggests
that his existence is simply a hoax.

Long as the public attention has been occupied by the
extraordinary personage from whose ambition we are supposed
to have so narrowly escaped, the subject seems to have lost
scarcely anything of its interest. We are still occupied in
recounting the exploits, discussing the character, inquiring into
the present situation, and even conjecturing as to the future
prospects of Napoleon Buonaparte.

Nor is this at all to be wondered at, if we consider the very
extraordinary nature of those exploits, and of that character;
their greatness and extensive importance, as well as the
unexampled strangeness of the events, and also that strong
additional stimulant, the mysterious uncertainty that hangs over
the character of the man. If it be doubtful whether any history
(exclusive of such as is confessedly fabulous) ever attributed to
its hero such a series of wonderful achievements compressed
into so small a space of time, it is certain that to no one were
ever assigned so many dissimilar characters.

It is true, indeed, that party-prejudices have drawn a
favourable and an unfavourable portrait of almost every eminent

179

man; but amidst all the diversities of colouring, something of the same general outline is always distinguishable. And even the virtues in the one description bear some resemblance to the vices of another: rashness, for instance, will be called courage, or courage, rashness; heroic firmness, and obstinate pride, will correspond in the two opposite descriptions; and in some leading features both will agree. Neither the friends nor the enemies of Philip of Macedon, or of Julius Cæsar, ever questioned their COURAGE, or their MILITARY SKILL.

With Buonaparte, however, it has been otherwise. This obscure Corsican adventurer, a man, according to some, of extraordinary talents and courage, according to others, of very moderate abilities, and a rank coward, advanced rapidly in the French army, obtained a high command, gained a series of important victories, and, elated by success, embarked in an expedition against Egypt; which was planned and conducted, according to some, with the most consummate skill, according to others, with the utmost wildness and folly: he was unsuccessful, however; and leaving the army in Egypt in a very distressed situation, he returned to France, and found the nation, or at least the army, so favourably disposed towards him, that he was enabled, with the utmost ease, to overthrow the existing government, and obtain for himself the supreme power; at first, under the modest appellation of Consul, but afterwards with the more sounding title of Emperor. While in possession of this power, he overthrew the most powerful coalitions of the other European States against him; and though driven from the sea by the British fleets, overran nearly the whole continent, triumphant; finishing a war, not unfrequently, in a single campaign, he entered the capitals of most of the hostile potentates, deposed and created Kings at his pleasure, and appeared the virtual sovereign of the chief part of the continent, from the frontiers of Spain to those of Russia. Even those countries we find him invading with prodigious armies, defeating their forces, penetrating to their capitals, and threatening their total subjugation. But at Moscow his progress is stopped: a winter of unusual severity, co-operating with the efforts of the Russians, totally destroys his enormous host: and the German sovereigns throw off the yoke, and combine to oppose him. He raises another vast army, which is also ruined at Leipsic; and again another, with which, like a second Antæus, he for some time maintains himself in France; but is finally defeated, deposed, and banished to the island of Elba, of which the sovereignty is conferred on him. Thence he returns, in about nine months, at the head of 600 men, to attempt the deposition of King Louis, who had been peaceably recalled; the French nation declare in his favour, and he is reinstated without a struggle. He raises another great army to oppose the allied powers, which is totally defeated at Waterloo; he is a second time deposed, surrenders to the British, and is placed in confinement at the island of St. Helena. Such is the outline of the eventful history presented to us; in the detail of which, however, there is almost every conceivable variety of statement; while the motives and conduct of the chief actor are involved in still greater doubt, and the subject of still more eager controversy.

In the midst of these controversies, the preliminary question, concerning the existence of this extraordinary personage, seems never to have occurred to any one as a matter of doubt; and to show even the smallest hesitation in admitting it, would probably be regarded as an excess of scepticism; on the ground that this point has always been taken for granted by the disputants on all sides, being indeed implied by the very nature of their disputes.

But is it in fact found that undisputed points are always such as have been the most carefully examined as to the evidence on which they rest? that facts or principles which are taken for granted, without controversy, as the common basis of opposite opinions, are always themselves established on sufficient grounds? On the contrary, is not any such fundamental point, from the very circumstance of its being taken for granted at once, and the attention drawn off to some other question, likely to be admitted on insufficient evidence, and the flaws in that evidence overlooked?

Experience will teach us that such instances often occur: witness the well-known anecdote of the Royal Society; to whom King Charles II. proposed as a question, whence it is that a vessel of water receives no addition of weight from a live fish being put into it, though it does, if the fish be dead. Various solutions, of great ingenuity, were proposed, discussed, objected to, and defended; nor was it till they had been long bewildered in the inquiry, that it occurred to them to try the experiment; by which they at once ascertained that the phenomenon which they were striving to account for,—which was the acknowledged basis and substratum, as it were, of their debates,—had no existence but in the invention of the witty monarch.[1]

Another instance of the same kind is so very remarkable that I cannot forbear mentioning it. It was objected to the system of Copernicus when first brought forward, that if the earth turned on its axis, as he represented, a stone dropped from the summit of a tower would not fall at the foot of it, but at a great distance to the west; in the same manner as a stone dropped from the mast-head of a ship in full sail, does not fall at the foot of the mast, but towards the stern. To this it was answered, that a stone being a part of the earth obeys the same laws, and moves with it; whereas, it is no part of the ship; of which, consequently, its motion is independent. This solution was admitted by some, but opposed by others; and the controversy went on with spirit; nor was it till one hundred years after the death of Copernicus, that the experiment being tried, it was ascertained that the stone thus dropped from the head of the mast does fall at the foot of it![2]

Let it be observed that I am not now impugning any one particular narrative; but merely showing generally, that what is unquestioned is not necessarily unquestionable; since men will often, at the very moment when they are accurately sifting the evidence of some disputed point, admit hastily, and on the most insufficient grounds, what they have been accustomed to see taken for granted.

The celebrated Hume[3] has pointed out, also, the readiness with which men believe, on very slight evidence, any story that pleases their imagination by its admirable and marvellous character. Such hasty credulity, however, as he well remarks, is utterly unworthy of a philosophical mind; which should rather suspend its judgment the more, in proportion to the strangeness of the account, and yield to none but the most decisive and unimpeachable proofs.

Let it, then, be allowed us, as is surely reasonable, just to inquire, with respect to the extraordinary story I have been speaking of, on what evidence we believe it. We shall be told that it is notorious; i.e., in plain English, it is very much talked about. But as the generality of those who talk about Buonaparte do not even pretend to speak from their own authority, but merely to repeat what they have casually heard, we cannot reckon them as, in any degree, witnesses; but must allow ninety-nine hundredths of what we are told to be mere hearsay, which would not be at all the more worthy of credit even if it were repeated by ten times as many more. As for those who profess to have personally known Napoleon Buonaparte, and to have themselves witnessed his transactions, I write not for them. If any such there be, who are inwardly conscious of the truth of all they relate, I have nothing to say to them, but to beg that they will be tolerant and charitable towards their neighbours, who have not the same means of ascertaining the truth, and who may well be excused for remaining doubtful about such extraordinary events, till most unanswerable proofs shall be adduced. "I would not have believed such a thing, if I had not seen it," is a common preface or appendix to a narrative of marvels; and usually calls forth from an intelligent hearer the appropriate answer, "no more will I."

Let us, however, endeavour to trace up some of this hearsay evidence as far towards its source as we are able. Most persons would refer to the newspapers as the authority from which their knowledge on the subject was derived; so that, generally speaking, we may say it is on the testimony of the newspapers that men believe in the existence and exploits of Napoleon Buonaparte.

It is rather a remarkable circumstance, that it is common to hear Englishmen speak of the impudent fabrications of foreign newspapers, and express wonder that any one can be found to credit them; while they conceive that, in this favoured land, the liberty of the press is a sufficient security for veracity. It is true they often speak contemptuously of such "newspaper-stories" as last but a short time; indeed they continually see them contradicted within a day or two in the same paper, or their falsity detected by some journal of an opposite party; but still whatever is long adhered to and often repeated, especially if it also appear in several different papers (and this, though they notoriously copy from one another), is almost sure to be generally believed. Whence this high respect which is practically paid to newspaper authority? Do men think, that because a witness has been perpetually detected in falsehood, he may therefore be the more safely believed whenever he is not detected? or does adherence to a story, and frequent repetition of it, render it the more credible? On the contrary, is it not a common remark in other cases, that a liar will generally stand to and reiterate what he has once said, merely because he has said it?

Let us, if possible, divest ourselves of this superstitious veneration for everything that appears "in print," and examine a little more systematically the evidence which is adduced.

I suppose it will not be denied that the three following are among the most important points to be ascertained, in deciding on the credibility of witnesses; first, whether they have the means of gaining correct information; secondly, whether they have any interest in concealing truth, or propagating falsehood; and, thirdly, whether they agree in their testimony. Let us examine the present witnesses upon all these points.

First, what means have the editors of newspapers for giving correct information? We know not, except from their own statements. Besides what is copied from other journals, foreign or British, (which is usually more than three-fourths of the news published,)[4] they profess to refer to the authority of certain "private correspondents" abroad; who these correspondents are, what means they have of obtaining information, or whether they exist at all, we have no way of ascertaining. We find ourselves in the condition of the Hindoos, who are told by their priests that the earth stands on an elephant, and the elephant on a tortoise; but are left to find out for themselves what the tortoise stands on, or whether it stands on anything at all.

So much for our clear knowledge of the means of information possessed by these witnesses; next, for the grounds on which we are to calculate on their veracity.

Have they not a manifest interest in circulating the wonderful accounts of Napoleon Buonaparte and his achievements, whether true or false? Few would read newspapers if they did not sometimes find wonderful or important news in them; and we may safely say that no subject was ever found so inexhaustibly interesting as the present.

It may be urged, however, that there are several adverse political parties, of which the various public prints are respectively the organs, and who would not fail to expose each other's fabrications.[5]

Doubtless they would, if they could do so without at the same time exposing their own; but identity of interests may induce a community of operations up to a certain point. And let it be observed that the object of contention between these rival parties is, who shall have the administration of public affairs, the control of public expenditure, and the disposal of places: the question, I say, is, not whether the people shall be governed or not, but, by which party they shall be governed;—not whether the taxes shall be paid or not, but who shall receive them. Now, it must be admitted that Buonaparte is a political bugbear, most convenient to any administration: "if you do not adopt our measures and reject those of our opponents, Buonaparte will be sure to prevail over you; if you do not submit to the Government, at least under our administration, this formidable enemy will take advantage of your insubordination, to conquer and enslave you: pay your taxes cheerfully, or the tremendous Buonaparte will take all from you." Buonaparte, in short, was the burden of every song; his redoubted name was the charm which always succeeded in unloosing the purse-strings of the nation. And let us not be too sure,[6] safe as we now think ourselves, that some occasion may not occur for again producing on the stage so useful a personage: it is not merely to naughty children in the nursery that the threat of being "given to Buonaparte" has proved effectual.

It is surely probable, therefore, that, with an object substantially the same, all parties may have availed themselves of one common instrument. It is not necessary to suppose that for this purpose they secretly entered into a formal agreement; though, by the way, there are reports afloat, that the editors of the Courier and Morning Chronicle hold amicable consultations as to the conduct of their public warfare: I will not take upon me to say that this is incredible; but at any rate it is not necessary for the establishment of the probability I contend for. Neither again would I imply that all newspaper editors are utterers of forged stories, "knowing them to be forged;" most likely the great majority of them publish what they find in other papers with the same simplicity that their readers peruse it; and therefore, it must be observed, are not at all more proper than their readers to be cited as authorities.

Still it will be said, that unless we suppose a regularly preconcerted plan, we must at least expect to find great discrepancies in the accounts published. Though they might adopt the general outline of facts from one another, they would have to fill up the detail for themselves; and in this, therefore, we should meet with infinite and irreconcilable variety.

Now this is precisely the point I am tending to; for the fact exactly accords with the above supposition; the discordance and mutual contradictions of these witnesses being such as would alone throw a considerable shade of doubt over their testimony. It is not in minute circumstances alone that the discrepancy appears, such as might be expected to appear in a narrative substantially true; but in very great and leading transactions, and such as are very intimately connected with the supposed hero. For instance, it is by no means agreed whether Buonaparte led in person the celebrated charge over the bridge of Lodi, (for celebrated it certainly is, as well as the siege of Troy, whether either event ever really took place or no,) or was safe in the rear, while Augereau performed the exploit. The same doubt hangs over the charge of the French cavalry at Waterloo. The peasant Lacoste, who professed to have been Buonaparte's guide on the day of battle, and who earned a fortune by detailing over and over again to visitors all the particulars of what the great man said and did up to the moment of flight,—this same Lacoste has been suspected by others, besides me, of having never even been near the great man, and having fabricated the whole story for the sake of making a gain of the credulity of travellers. In the accounts that are the extant of the battle itself, published by persons professing to have been present, the reader will find that there is a discrepancy of three or four hours as to the time when the battle began!—a battle, be it remembered, not fought with javelins and arrows, like those of the ancients, in which one part of a large army might be engaged, whilst a distant portion of the same army knew nothing of it; but a battle commencing (if indeed it were ever fought at all) with the firing of cannon, which, would have announced pretty loudly what was going on.

It is no less uncertain whether or no this strange personage poisoned in Egypt an hospital—full of his own soldiers, and butchered in cold blood a garrison that had surrendered. But not to multiply instances; the battle of Borodino, which is represented as one of the greatest ever fought, was unequivocally claimed as a victory by both parties; nor is the question decided at this day. We have official accounts on both sides, circumstantially detailed, in the names of supposed respectable persons, professing to have been present on the spot; yet totally irreconcilable. Both these accounts may be false; but since one of them must be false, that one (it is no matter which we suppose) proves incontrovertibly this important maxim: that it is possible for a narrative—however circumstantial—however steadily maintained—however public, and however important, the events it relates—however grave the authority on which it is published—to be nevertheless an entire fabrication!

Many of the events which have been recorded were probably believed much the more readily and firmly, from the apparent caution and hesitation with which they were at first published— the vehement contradiction in our papers of many pretended French accounts—and the abuse lavished upon them for falsehood, exaggeration, and gasconade. But is it not possible— is it not, indeed, perfectly natural—that the publishers even of known falsehood should assume this cautious demeanour, and this abhorrence of exaggeration, in order the more easily to gain credit? Is it not also very possible, that those who actually believed what they published, may have suspected mere exaggeration in stories which were entire fictions? Many men have that sort of simplicity, that they think themselves quite secure against being deceived, provided they believe only part of the story they hear; when perhaps the whole is equally false. So that perhaps these simple-hearted editors, who were so vehement against lying bulletins, and so wary in announcing their great news, were in the condition of a clown, who thinks he has bought a great bargain of a Jew because he has beat down the price perhaps from a guinea to a crown, for some article that is not really worth a groat.

With respect to the character of Buonaparte, the dissonance is, if possible, still greater. According to some, he was a wise, humane, magnanimous hero; others paint him as a monster of cruelty, meanness, and perfidy: some, even of those who are most inveterate against him, speak very highly of his political and military ability: others place him on the very verge of insanity. But allowing that all this may be the colouring of party-prejudice, (which surely is allowing a great deal,) there is one point to which such a solution will hardly apply: if there be anything that can be clearly ascertained in history, one would think it must be the personal courage of a military man; yet here we are as much at a loss as ever; at the very same times, and on the same occasions, he is described by different writers as a man of undaunted intrepidity, and as an absolute poltroon.

What, then, are we to believe? If we are disposed to credit all that is told us, we must believe in the existence not only of one, but of two or three Buonapartes; if we admit nothing but what is well authenticated, we shall be compelled to doubt of the existence of any.[7] It appears, then, that those on whose testimony the existence and actions of Buonaparte are generally believed, fail in ALL the most essential points on which the credibility of witnesses depends: first, we have no assurance that they have access to correct information; secondly, they have an apparent interest in propagating falsehood; and, thirdly, they palpably contradict each other in the most important points.

Another circumstance which throws additional suspicion on these tales is, that the whig-party, as they are called—the warm advocates for liberty, and opposers of the encroachments of monarchical power—have for some time past strenuously espoused the cause and vindicated the character of Buonaparte, who is represented by all as having been, if not a tyrant, at least an absolute despot. One of the most forward in this cause is a gentleman, who once stood foremost in holding up this very man to public execration—who first published, and long maintained against popular incredulity, the accounts of his atrocities in Egypt. Now that such a course should be adopted for party-purposes; by those who are aware that the whole story is a fiction, and the hero of it imaginary, seems not very incredible; but if they believed in the real existence of this despot, I cannot conceive how they could so forsake their principles as to

189

advocate his cause, and eulogize his character.

Besides the many strange and improbable circumstances in the history of Buonaparte that have been already noticed, there are many others, two of which it may be worth while to advert to. One of the most incredible is the received account of the persons known as the "Détenus." It is well known that a great number of English gentlemen passed many years, in the early part of the present century, abroad;—by their own account, in France. Their statement was, that while travelling in that country for their amusement, as peaceable tourists, they were, on the sudden breaking out of a war, seized by this terrible Buonaparte, and kept prisoners for about twelve years, contrary to all the usages of civilized nations—to all principles of justice, of humanity, of enlightened policy; many of them thus wasting in captivity the most important portion of their lives, and having all their prospects blighted.

Now whether these persons were in reality exiles by choice, for the sake of keeping out of the way of creditors, or of enjoying the society of those they preferred to their own domestic circle, I do not venture to conjecture. But let the reader consider whether any conjecture can be more improbable than the statement actually made.

It is, indeed, credible that ambition may prompt an unscrupulous man to make the most enormous sacrifices of human life, and to perpetrate the most atrocious crimes, for the advancement of his views of conquest. But that this great man—as he is usually reckoned even by adversaries—this hero according to some—this illustrious warrior, and mighty sovereign—should have stooped to be guilty of an act of mean and petty malice worthy of a spiteful old woman,—a piece of paltry cruelty which could not at all conduce to his success in the war, or produce any effect except to degrade his country, and exasperate ours;—this, surely, is quite incredible. "Pizarro," says Elvira in Kotzebue's play, "if not always justly, at least act always greatly."

But a still more wonderful circumstance connected with this transaction remains behind. A large portion of the English nation, and among these the whole of the Whig party, are said to have expressed the most vehement indignation, mingled with compassion, at the banishment from Europe, and confinement in St. Helena, of this great man. No considerations of regard for the peace and security of our own country, no dread of the power of so able and indefatigable a warrior, and so inveterate an enemy, should have induced us, they thought, to subject this formidable personage to a confinement, which was far less severe than that to which he was said to have subjected such numbers of our countrymen, the harmless non-belligerent travellers, whom (according to the story) he kidnapped in France, with no object but to gratify the basest and most unmanly spite.

But that there is no truth in that story, and that it was not believed by those who manifested so much sympathy and indignation on this great man's account, is sufficiently proved by that very sympathy and indignation.

There are again other striking improbabilities connected with the Polish nation in the history before us. Buonaparte is represented as having always expressed the strongest sympathy with that ill-used people; and they, as being devotedly attached to him, and fighting with the utmost fidelity and bravery in his armies, in which some of them attained high commands. Now he had it manifestly in his power at one period (according to the received accounts), with a stroke of his pen, to re-establish Poland as an independent state. For, in his last Russian war, he had complete occupation of the country (of which the population was perfectly friendly); the Russian portion of it was his by right of conquest; and Austria and Prussia, then his allies, and almost his subjects, would gladly have resigned their portions in exchange for some of the provinces they had ceded to France, and which were, to him, of little value, but, to them, important. And, indeed, Prussia was (as we are told) so thoroughly humbled and weakened that he might easily have enforced the cession of Prussian-Poland, even without any compensation. And the re-establishment of the Polish kingdom would have been as evidently politic as it was reasonable. The independence of a faithful and devoted ally, at enmity with the surrounding nations—the very nations that were the most likely to combine (as they often had done) against him,—this would have given him, at no cost, a kind of strong garrison to maintain his power, and keep his enemies in check.

Yet this most obvious step, the history tells us, he did not take; but made flattering speeches to the Poles, used their services, and did nothing for them!

This is, alone, sufficiently improbable. But we are required moreover to believe that the Poles,—instead of execrating this man, who had done them the unpardonable wrong of wantonly disappointing the expectations he had, for his own purposes, excited, thus adding treachery to ingratitude—instead of this, continued to the last as much devoted to him as ever, and even now idolize his memory! We are to believe, in short, that this Buonaparte, not only in his own conduct and adventures violated all the established rules of probability, but also caused all other persons, as many as came in contact with him, to act as no mortals ever did act before: may we not add, as no mortals ever did act at all?

Many other improbabilities might be added to the list, and will be found in the complete edition of that history, from which some extracts will be presently given, and which has been published (under the title of "Historic Certainties") by Aristarchus Newlight, with a learned commentary (not, indeed, adopting the views contained in these pages, but) quite equal in ingenuity to a late work on the "Hebrew Monarchy."

After all, it may be expected that many who perceive the force of these objections, will yet be loth to think it possible that they and the public at large can have been so long and so greatly imposed upon. And thus it is that the magnitude and boldness of a fraud becomes its best support. The millions who for so many ages have believed in Mahomet or Brahma, lean as it were on each other for support; and not having vigour of mind enough boldly to throw off vulgar prejudices, and dare be wiser than the multitude, persuade themselves that what so many have acknowledged must be true. But I call on those who boast their philosophical freedom of thought, and would fain tread in the steps of Hume and other inquirers of the like exalted and speculative genius, to follow up fairly and fully their own principles, and, throwing off the shackles of authority, to examine carefully the evidence of whatever is proposed to them, before they admit its truth.

That even in this enlightened age, as it is called, a whole nation may be egregiously imposed upon, even in matters which intimately concern them, may be proved (if it has not been already proved) by the following instance: it was stated in the newspapers, that, a month after the battle of Trafalgar, an English officer, who had been a prisoner of war, and was exchanged, returned to this country from France, and beginning to condole with his countrymen on the terrible defeat they had sustained, was infinitely astonished to learn that the battle of Trafalgar was a splendid victory. He had been assured, he said, that in that battle the English had been totally defeated; and the French were fully and universally persuaded that such was the fact. Now if this report of the belief of the French nation was not true, the British Public were completely imposed upon; if it were true, then both nations were, at the same time, rejoicing in the event of the same battle, as a signal victory to themselves; and consequently one or other, at least, of these nations must have been the dupes of their government: for if the battle was never fought at all, or was not decisive on either side, in that case both parties were deceived. This instance, I conceive, is absolutely demonstrative of the point in question.

"But what shall we say to the testimony of those many respectable persons who went to Plymouth on purpose, and saw Buonaparte with their own eyes? must they not trust their senses?" I would not disparage either the eyesight or the veracity of these gentlemen. I am ready to allow that they went to Plymouth for the purpose of seeing Buonaparte; nay, more, that they actually rowed out into the harbour in a boat, and came alongside of a man-of-war, on whose deck they saw a man in a cocked hat, who, they were told, was Buonaparte. This is the utmost point to which their testimony goes; how they ascertained that this man in the cocked hat had gone through all the marvellous and romantic adventures with which we have so long been amused, we are not told. Did they perceive in his physiognomy, his true name, and authentic history? Truly this evidence is such as country people give one for a story of apparitions; if you discover any signs of incredulity, they triumphantly show the very house which the ghost haunted, the identical dark corner where it used to vanish, and perhaps even the tombstone of the person whose death it foretold. Jack Cade's nobility was supported by the same irresistible kind of evidence: having asserted that the eldest son of Edmund Mortimer, Earl of March, was stolen by a beggar-woman, "became a bricklayer when he came to age," and was the father of the supposed Jack Cade; one of his companions confirms the story, by saying, "Sir, he made a chimney in my father's house, and the bricks are alive at this day to testify it; therefore, deny it not."

Much of the same kind is the testimony of our brave countrymen, who are ready to produce the scars they received in fighting against this terrible Buonaparte. That they fought and were wounded, they may safely testify; and probably they no less firmly believe what they were told respecting the cause in which they fought: it would have been a high breach of discipline to doubt it; and they, I conceive, are men better skilled in handling a musket, than in sifting evidence, and detecting imposture. But I defy any one of them to come forward and declare, on his own knowledge, what was the cause in which he fought,—under whose commands the opposed generals acted,—and whether the person who issued those commands did really perform the mighty achievements we are told of.

Let those, then, who pretend to philosophical freedom of inquiry,—who scorn to rest their opinions on popular belief, and to shelter themselves under the example of the unthinking multitude, consider carefully, each one for himself, what is the evidence proposed to himself in particular, for the existence of such a person as Napoleon Buonaparte:—I do not mean, whether there ever was a person bearing that name, for that is a question of no consequence; but whether any such person ever performed all the wonderful things attributed to him;—let him then weigh well the objections to that evidence, (of which I have given but a hasty and imperfect sketch,) and if he then finds it amount to anything more than a probability, I have only to congratulate him on his easy faith.

But the same testimony which would have great weight in establishing a thing intrinsically probable, will lose part of this weight in proportion as the matter attested is improbable; and if adduced in support of anything that is at variance with uniform experience,[8] will be rejected at once by all sound reasoners. Let us then consider what sort of a story it is that is proposed to our acceptance. How grossly contradictory are the reports of the different authorities, I have already remarked: but consider, by itself, the story told by any one of them; it carries an air of fiction and romance on the very face of it. All the events are great, and splendid, and marvellous;[9] great armies,—great victories,— great frosts,—great reverses,—"hair-breadth 'scapes,"—empires subverted in a few days; everything happened in defiance of political calculations, and in opposition to the experience of past times; everything upon that grand scale, so common in Epic Poetry, so rare in real life; and thus calculated to strike the imagination of the vulgar, and to remind the sober-thinking few of the Arabian Nights. Every event, too, has that roundness and completeness which is so characteristic of fiction; nothing is done by halves; we have complete victories,—total overthrows, entire subversion of empires,—perfect re-establishments of them,—crowded upon us in rapid succession. To enumerate the improbabilities of each of the several parts of this history, would fill volumes; but they are so fresh in every one's memory, that there is no need of such a detail: let any judicious man, not ignorant of history and of human nature, revolve them in his mind, and consider how far they are conformable to Experience,[10] our best and only sure guide. In vain will he seek in history for something similar to this wonderful Buonaparte; "nought but himself can be his parallel."

Will the conquests of Alexander be compared with his? They were effected over a rabble of effeminate, undisciplined barbarians; else his progress would hardly have been so rapid: witness his father Philip, who was much longer occupied in subduing the comparatively insignificant territory of the warlike and civilized Greeks, notwithstanding their being divided into numerous petty States, whose mutual jealousy enabled him to contend with them separately. But the Greeks had never made such progress in arts and arms as the great and powerful States of Europe, which Buonaparte is represented as so speedily overpowering. His empire has been compared to the Roman: mark the contrast; he gains in a few years, that dominion, or at least control, over Germany, wealthy, civilized, and powerful, which the Romans in the plenitude of their power, could not obtain, during a struggle of as many centuries, against the ignorant half-savages who then possessed it; of whom Tacitus remarks, that, up to his own time they had been "triumphed over rather than conquered."

Another peculiar circumstance in the history of this extraordinary personage is, that when it Is found convenient to represent him as defeated, though he is by no means defeated by halves, but involved in much more sudden and total ruin than the personages of real history usually meet with; yet, if it is thought fit he should be restored, it is done as quickly and completely as if Merlin's rod had been employed. He enters Russia with a prodigious army, which is totally ruined by an unprecedented hard winter; (everything relating to this man is prodigious and unprecedented;) yet in a few months we find him intrusted with another great army in Germany, which is also totally ruined at Leipsic; making, inclusive of the Egyptian, the third great army thus totally lost: yet the French are so good-natured as to furnish him with another sufficient to make a formidable stand in France; he is, however, conquered, and presented with the sovereignty of Elba; (surely, by the bye, some more probable way might have been found of disposing of him, till again wanted, than to place him thus on the very verge of his ancient dominions;) thence he returns to France, where he is received with open arms, and enabled to lose a fifth great army at Waterloo; yet so eager were these people to be a sixth time led to destruction, that it was found necessary to confine him in an island some thousand miles off, and to quarter foreign troops upon them, lest they should make an insurrection in his favour?[11] Does any one believe all this, and yet refuse to believe a miracle? Or rather, what is this but a miracle? Is it not a violation of the laws of nature? for surely there are moral laws of nature as well as physical; which though more liable to exceptions in this or that particular case, are no less true as general rules than the laws of matter, and therefore cannot be violated and contradicted beyond a certain point, without a miracle.[12]

Nay, there is this additional circumstance which renders the contradiction of Experience more glaring in this case than in that of the miraculous histories which ingenious sceptics have held up to contempt: all the advocates of miracles admit that they are rare exceptions to the general course of nature; but contend that they must needs be so, on account of the rarity of those extraordinary occasions which are the reason of their being performed: a Miracle, they say, does not happen every day, because a Revelation is not given every day. It would be foreign to the present purpose to seek for arguments against this answer; I leave it to those who are engaged in the controversy, to find a reply to it; but my present object is, to point out that this solution does not at all apply in the present case. Where is the peculiarity of the occasion? What sufficient reason is there for a series of events occurring in the eighteenth and nineteenth centuries, which never took place before? Was Europe at that period peculiarly weak, and in a state of barbarism, that one man could achieve such conquests, and acquire such a vast empire? On the contrary, she was flourishing in the height of strength and civilization. Can the persevering attachment and blind devotedness of the French to this man, be accounted for by his being the descendant of a long line of kings, whose race was hallowed by hereditary veneration? No; we are told he was a low-born usurper, and not even a Frenchman! Is it that he was a good and kind sovereign? He is represented not only as an imperious and merciless despot, but as most wantonly careless of the lives of his soldiers. Could the French army and people have failed to hear from the wretched survivors of his supposed Russian expedition, how they had left the corpses of above 100,000 of their comrades bleaching on the snow-drifts of that dismal country, whither his mad ambition had conducted him, and where his selfish cowardice had deserted them? Wherever we turn to seek for circumstances that may help to account for the events of this incredible story, we only meet with such as aggravate its improbability.[13] Had it been told of some distant country, at a remote period, we could not have told what peculiar circumstances there might have been to render probable what seems to us most strange; and yet in that case every philosophical sceptic, every free-thinking speculator, would instantly have rejected such a history, as utterly unworthy of credit. What, for instance, would the great Hume, or any of the philosophers of his school, have said, if they had found in the antique records of any nation, such a passage as this? "There was a certain man of Corsica, whose name was Napoleon, and he was one of the chief captains of the host of the French; and he gathered together an army, and went and fought against Egypt: but when the king of Britain heard thereof, he sent ships of war and valiant men to fight against the French in Egypt. So they warred against them, and prevailed, and strengthened the hands of the rulers of the land against the French, and drave away Napoleon from before the city of Acre. Then Napoleon left the captains and the army that were in Egypt, and fled, and returned back to France. So the French people, took Napoleon, and made him ruler over them, and he became exceeding great, insomuch that there was none like him of all that had ruled over France before."

What, I say, would Hume have thought of this, especially if he had been told that it was at this day generally credited? Would he not have confessed that he had been mistaken in supposing there was a peculiarly blind credulity and prejudice in favour of everything that is accounted sacred;"[14] for that, since even professed sceptics swallow implicitly such a story as this, it appears there must be a still blinder prejudice in favour of everything that is not accounted sacred?

Suppose, again, we found in this history such passages as the following: "And it came to pass after these things that Napoleon strengthened himself, and gathered together another host instead of that which he had lost, and went and warred against the Prussians, and the Russians, and the Austrians, and all the rulers of the north country, which were confederate against him. And the ruler of Sweden, also, which was a Frenchman, warred against Napoleon. So they went forth, and fought against the French in the plain of Leipsic. And the French were discomfited before their enemies, and fled, and came to the rivers which are behind Leipsic, and essayed to pass over, that they might escape out of the hand of their enemies; but they could not, for Napoleon had broken down the bridges: so the people of the north countries came upon them, and smote them with a very grievous slaughter."

"Then the ruler of Austria and all the rulers of the north countries sent messengers unto Napoleon to speak peaceably unto him, saying, Why should there be war between us any more? Now Napoleon had put away his wife, and taken the daughter of the ruler of Austria to wife. So all the counsellors of Napoleon came and stood before him, and said, Behold now these kings are merciful kings; do even as they say unto thee; knowest thou not yet that France is destroyed? But he spake roughly unto his counsellors, and drave them, out from his presence, neither would he hearken unto their voice. And when all the kings saw that, they warred against France, and smote it with the edge of the sword, and came near to Paris, which is the royal city, to take it: so the men of Paris went out, and delivered up the city to them. Then those kings spake kindly unto the men of Paris, saying, Be of good cheer, there shall no harm happen unto you. Then were the men of Paris glad, and said, Napoleon is a tyrant; he shall no more rule over us. Also all the princes, the judges, the counsellors, and the captains whom Napoleon had raised up even from the lowest of the people, sent unto Lewis the brother of King Lewis, whom they had slain, and made him king over France."

"And when Napoleon saw that the kingdom was departed from him, he said unto the rulers which came against him, Let me, I pray you, give the kingdom unto my son: but they would not hearken unto him. Then he spake yet again, saying, Let me, I pray you, go and live in the island of Elba, which is over against Italy, nigh unto the coast of France; and ye shall give me an allowance for me and my household, and the land of Elba also for a possession. So they made him ruler of Elba."

"In those days the Pope returned unto his own land. Now the French, and divers other nations of Europe, are servants of the Pope, and hold him in reverence; but he is an abomination unto the Britons, and to the Prussians, and to the Russians, and to the Swedes. Howbeit the French had taken away all his lands, and robbed him of all that he had, and carried him away captive into France. But when the Britons, and the Prussians, and the Russians, and the Swedes, and the rest of the nations that were confederate against France, came thither, they caused the

French to set the Pope at liberty, and to restore all his goods that they had taken; likewise they gave him back all his possessions; and he went home in peace, and ruled over his own city as in times past."

"And it came to pass when Napoleon had not yet been a full year at Elba, that he said unto his men of war that clave unto him, Go to, let us go back to France, and fight against King Lewis, and thrust him out from being king. So he departed, he and six hundred men with him that drew the sword, and warred against King Lewis. Then all the men of Belial gathered themselves together, and said, God save Napoleon. And when Lewis saw that, he fled, and gat him into the land of Batavia: and Napoleon ruled over France," &c. &c. &c.[15]

Now if a free-thinking philosopher—one of those who advocate the cause of unbiassed reason, and despise pretended revelations—were to meet with such a tissue of absurdities as this in an old Jewish record, would he not reject it at once as too palpable an imposture[16]

Let it be borne in mind that Hume (as I have above remarked) continually employs the term "miracle" and "prodigy" to signify anything that is highly improbable and extraordinary to deserve even any inquiry into its evidence? Is that credible then of the civilized Europeans now, which could not, if reported of the semi-barbarous Jews 3000 years ago, be established by any testimony? Will it be answered, that "there is nothing supernatural in all this?" Why is it, then, that you object to what is supernatural—that you reject every account of miracles—if not because they are improbable? Surely then a story equally or still more improbable, is not to be implicitly received, merely on the ground that it is not miraculous: though in fact, as I have already shown from Hume's authority, it is really miraculous. The opposition to Experience has been proved to be as complete in this case, as in what are commonly called miracles; and the reasons assigned for that contrariety by the defenders of them, cannot be pleaded in the present instance.

If then philosophers, who reject every wonderful story that is maintained by priests, are yet found ready to believe everything else, however improbable, they will surely lay themselves open to the accusation brought against them of being unduly prejudiced against whatever relates to religion.

There is one more circumstance which I cannot forbear mentioning, because it so much adds to the air of fiction which pervades every part of this marvellous tale; and that is, the nationality of it.[17]

Buonaparte prevailed over all the hostile States in turn, except England; in the zenith of his power, his fleets were swept from the sea, by England; his troops always defeat an equal, and frequently even a superior number of those of any other nation, except the English; and with them it is just the reverse; twice, and twice only, he is personally engaged against an English commander, and both times he is totally defeated; at Acre, and at Waterloo; and to crown all, England finally crushes this tremendous power, which had so long kept the continent in subjection or in alarm; and to the English he surrenders himself prisoner! Thoroughly national, to be sure! It may be all very true; but I would only ask, if a story had been fabricated for the express purpose of amusing the English nation, could it have been contrived more ingeniously? It would do admirably for an epic poem; and indeed bears a considerable resemblance to the Iliad and the Æneid; in which Achilles and the Greeks, Æneas and the Trojans, (the ancestors of the Romans) are so studiously held up to admiration. Buonaparte's exploits seem magnified in order to enhance the glory of his conquerors; just as Hector is allowed to triumph during the absence of Achilles, merely to give additional splendour to his overthrow by the arm of that invincible hero. Would not this circumstance alone render a history rather suspicious in the eyes of an acute critic, even if it were not filled with such gross improbabilities; and induce him to suspend his judgment, till very satisfactory evidence (far stronger than can be found in this case) should be produced?

Is it then too much to demand of the wary academic[18] a suspension of judgment as to the "life and adventures of Napoleon Buonaparte?" I do not pretend to decide positively that there is not, nor ever was, any such person; but merely to propose it as a doubtful point, and one the more deserving of careful investigation, from the very circumstance of its having hitherto been admitted without inquiry. Far less would I undertake to decide what is or has been the real state of affairs. He who points out the improbability of the current story, is not bound to suggest an hypothesis of his own;[19] though it may safely be affirmed, that it would be hard to invent any one more improbable than the received one. One may surely be allowed to hesitate in admitting the stories which the ancient poets tell, of earthquakes and volcanic eruptions being caused by imprisoned giants, without being called upon satisfactorily to account for those phenomena.

Amidst the defect of valid evidence under which, as I have already shown, we labour in the present instance, it is hardly possible to offer more than here and there a probable conjecture; or to pronounce how much may be true, and how much fictitious, in the accounts presented to us. For, it is to be observed that this case is much more open to sceptical doubts even than some miraculous histories; since some of them are of such a nature that you cannot consistently admit a part and reject the rest; but are bound, if you are satisfied as to the reality of any one miracle, to embrace the whole system; so that it is necessary for the sceptic to impeach the evidence of all of them, separately, and collectively: whereas, here, each single point requires to be established separately, since no one of them authenticates the rest. Supposing there be a state-prisoner at St. Helena, (which, by the way, it is acknowledged many of the French disbelieve,) how do we know who he is, or why he is confined there? There have been state-prisoners before now, who were never guilty of subjugating half Europe, and whose offences have been very imperfectly ascertained. Admitting that there have been bloody wars going on for several years past, which is highly probable, it does not follow that the events of those wars were such as we have been told;—that Buonaparte was the author and conductor of them;—or that such a person ever existed. What disturbances may have taken place in the government of the French people, we, and even nineteen-twentieths of them, have no means of learning but from imperfect hearsay evidence; and how much credit they themselves attach to that evidence is very doubtful. This at least is certain: that a M. Berryer, a French advocate, has published memoirs, professing to record many of the events of the recent history of France, in which, among other things, he states his conviction that Buonaparte's escape from Elba was designed and contrived by the English Government.[20] And we are assured by many travellers that this was, and is, commonly reported in France.

Now that the French should believe the whole story about Buonaparte according to this version of it, does seem utterly incredible. Let any one suppose them seriously believing that we maintained for many years a desperate struggle against this formidable emperor of theirs, in the course of which we expended such an enormous amount of blood and treasure as is reported;—that we finally, after encountering enormous risks, succeeded in subduing him, and secured him in a place of safe exile;—and that, in less than a year after, we turned him out again, like a bag-fox,—or rather, a bag-lion,—for the sake of amusing ourselves by again staking all that was dear to us on the event of a doubtful and bloody battle, in which defeat must be ruinous, and victory, if obtained at all, must cost us many thousands of our best soldiers. Let any one force himself for a moment to conceive the French seriously believing such a mass of absurdity; and the inference must be that such a people must be prepared to believe anything. They might fancy their own country to abound not only with Napoleons, but with dragons and centaurs, and "men whose heads do grow beneath their shoulders," or anything else that any lunatic ever dreamt of. If we could suppose the French capable of such monstrous credulity as the above supposition would imply, it is plain their testimony must be altogether worthless.

But, on the other hand, suppose them to be aware that the British Government have been all along imposing on us, and it is quite natural that they should deride our credulity, and try whether there is anything too extravagant for us to swallow. And indeed, if Buonaparte was in fact altogether a phantom conjured up by the British Ministers, then it is true that his escape from Elba really was, as well as the rest of his exploits, a contrivance of theirs.

But whatever may be believed by the French relative to the recent occurrences, in their own country, and whatever may be the real character of these occurrences, of this at least we are well assured, that there have been numerous bloody wars with France under the dominion of the Bourbons: and we are now told that France is governed by a Bourbon king, of the name of Lewis, who professes to be in the twenty-third year of his reign. Let every one conjecture for himself. I am far from pretending to decide who may have been the governor or governors of the French nation, and the leaders of their armies, for several years past. Certain it is, that when men are indulging their inclination for the marvellous, they always show a strong propensity to accumulate upon one individual (real or imaginary) the exploits of many; besides multiplying and exaggerating these exploits a thousandfold. Thus, the expounders of the ancient mythology tell us there were several persons of the name of Hercules, (either originally bearing that appellation, or having it applied to them as an honour,) whose collective feats, after being dressed up in a sufficiently marvellous garb, were attributed to a single hero. Is it not just possible, that during the rage for words of Greek derivation, the title of "Napoleon," (Ναπολεων,) which signifies "Lion of the forest," may have been conferred by the popular voice on more than one favorite general, distinguished for irresistible valour? Is it not also possible that "Buona Parte"

205

may have been originally a sort of cant term applied to the "good (i.e., the bravest or most patriotic) part" of the French army, collectively; and have been afterwards mistaken for the proper name of an individual?[21] I do not profess to support this conjecture; but it is certain that such mistakes may and do occur. Some critics have supposed that the Athenians imagined Anastasis ("Resurrection") to be a new goddess, in whose cause Paul was preaching. Would it have been thought anything incredible if we had been told that the ancient Persians, who had no idea of any but a monarchical government, had supposed Aristocratia to be a queen of Sparta? But we need not confine ourselves to hypothetical cases; it is positively stated that the Hindoos at this day believe "the honourable East India Company" to be a venerable old lady of high dignity, residing in this country. The Germans, again, of the present day derive their name from a similar mistake: the first tribe of them who invaded Gaul[22] assumed the honourable title of "Ger-man" which signifies "warriors," (the words "war" and "guerre," as well as "man," which remains in our language unaltered, are evidently derived from the Teutonic,) and the Gauls applied this as a name to the whole race.

However, I merely throw out these conjectures without by any means contending that more plausible ones might not be suggested. But whatever supposition we adopt, or whether we adopt any, the objections to the commonly received accounts will remain in their full force, and imperiously demand the attention of the candid sceptic.

I call upon those, therefore, who profess themselves advocates of free inquiry—who disdain to be carried along with the stream of popular opinion, and who will listen to no testimony that runs counter to experience,—to follow up their own principles fairly and consistently. Let the same mode of argument be adopted in all cases alike; and then it can no longer be attributed to hostile prejudice, but to enlarged and philosophical views. If they have already rejected some histories, on the ground of their being strange and marvellous,—of their relating facts, unprecedented, and at variance with the established course of nature,—let them not give credit to another history which lies open to the very same objections,—the extraordinary and romantic tale we have been just considering. If they have discredited the testimony of witnesses, who are said at least to have been disinterested, and to have braved persecutions and death in support of their assertions,—can these philosophers consistently listen to and believe the testimony of those who avowedly get money by the tales they publish, and who do not even pretend that they incur any serious risk in case of being detected in a falsehood? If, in other cases, they have refused to listen to an account which has passed through many intermediate hands before it reaches them, and which is defended by those who have an interest in maintaining it; let them consider through how many, and what very suspicious hands, this story has arrived to them, without the possibility, as I have shown, of tracing it back to any decidedly authentic source, after all;—to any better authority, according to their own showing, than that of an unnamed and unknown foreign correspondent;—and likewise how strong an interest, in every way, those who have hitherto imposed on them, have in keeping up the imposture. Let them, in short, show themselves as ready to detect the cheats, and despise the fables of politicians as of priests.

But if they are still wedded to the popular belief in this point, let them be consistent enough to admit the same evidence in other cases which they yield to in this. If, after all that has been said, they cannot bring themselves to doubt of the existence of Napoleon Buonaparte, they must at least acknowledge that they do not apply to that question the same plan of reasoning which they have made use of in others; and they are consequently bound in reason and in honesty to renounce it altogether.

Postscript to the Third Edition

It may seem arrogant for an obscure and nameless individual to claim the glory of having put to death the most formidable of all recorded heroes. But a shadowy champion may be overthrown by a shadowy antagonist. Many a terrific spectre has been laid by the beams of a halfpenny candle. And if I have succeeded in making out, in the foregoing pages, a probable case of suspicion, it must, I think, be admitted, that there is some ground for my present boast, of having killed Napoleon Buonaparte.

Let but the circumstances of the case be considered. This mighty Emperor, who had been so long the bugbear of the civilized world, after having obtained successes and undergone reverses, such as never befel any (other at least) real potentate, was at length sentenced to confinement in the remote island of St. Helena: a measure which many persons wondered at, and many objected to, on various grounds; not unreasonably, supposing the illustrious exile to be a real person; but on the supposition of his being only a man of straw, the situation was exceedingly favourable for keeping him out of the way of impertinent curiosity, when not wanted, and for making him the foundation of any new plots that there might be occasion to conjure up.

About this juncture it was that the public attention was first invited, by these pages, to the question as to the real existence of Napoleon Buonaparte. They excited, it may be fairly supposed, along with much surprise and much censure, some degree of doubt, and probably of consequent inquiry. No fresh evidence, as far as I can learn, of the truth of the disputed points, was brought forward to dispel these doubts. We heard, however, of the most jealous precautions being used to prevent any intercourse between the formidable prisoner, and any stranger who, from motives of curiosity, might wish to visit him. The "man in the iron mask" could hardly have been more rigorously secluded: and we also heard various contradictory reports of conversations between him and the few who were allowed access to him; the falsehood and inconsistency of most of these reports being proved in contemporary publications.

At length, just about the time when the public scepticism respecting this extraordinary personage might be supposed to have risen to an alarming height, it was announced to us that he was dead! A stop was thus put, most opportunely, to all troublesome inquiries. I do not undertake to deny that such a person did live and die. That he was, and that he did, everything that is reported, we cannot believe, unless we consent to admit contradictory statements; but many of the events reported, however marvellous, are certainly not, when taken separately, physically impossible. But I would only entreat the candid reader to reflect what might naturally be expected, on the supposition of the surmises contained in the present work being well founded. Supposing the whole of the tale I have been considering to have been a fabrication, what would be the natural result of such attempt to excite inquiry into its truth? Evidently the shortest and most effectual mode of avoiding detection, would be to kill the phantom, and so get rid of him at once. A ready and decisive answer would thus be provided to any one in whom the foregoing arguments might have excited suspicions: "Sir, there can be no doubt that such a person existed, and performed what is related of him; and if you will just take a voyage to St. Helena, you may see with your own eyes,—not him, indeed, for he is no longer living,—but his tomb: and what evidence would you have that is more decisive?"

So much for his Death: as for his Life,—it is just published by an eminent writer: besides which, the shops will supply us with abundance of busts and prints of this great man; all striking likenesses—of one another. The most incredulous must be satisfied with this! "Stat magni NOMINIS umbra!"

KONX OMPAX.

Postscript to the Seventh Edition

Since the publication of the Sixth Edition of this work, the French nation, and the world at large, have obtained an additional evidence, to which I hope they will attach as much weight as it deserves, of the reality of the wonderful history I have been treating of. The Great Nation, among the many indications lately given of an heroic zeal like what Homer attributes to his Argive warriors, τίσασθαι ΕΛΈΝΗΣ ὁρμήματά τε στοναχάς τε, have formed and executed the design of bringing home for honourable interment the remains of their illustrious Chief.

How many persons have actually inspected these relics, I have not ascertained; but that a real coffin, containing real bones, was brought from St. Helena to France, I see no reason to disbelieve.

Whether future visitors to St. Helena will be shown merely the identical place in which Buonaparte was (said to have been) interred, or whether another set of real bones will be exhibited in that island, we have yet to learn.

This latter supposition is not very improbable. It was something of a credit to the island, an attraction to strangers, and a source of profit to some of the inhabitants, to possess so remarkable a relic; and this glory and advantage they must naturally wish to retain. If so, there seems no reason why they should not have a Buonaparte of their own; for there is, I believe, no doubt that there are, or were, several Museums in England, which, among other curiosities, boasted, each, of a genuine skull of Oliver Cromwell.

Perhaps, therefore, we shall hear of several well authenticated skulls of Buonaparte also, in the collections of different virtuosos, all of whom (especially those in whose own crania the "organ of wonder" is the most largely developed) will doubtless derive equal satisfaction from the relics they respectively possess.

Postscript to the Ninth Edition

The Public has been of late much interested and not a little bewildered, by the accounts of many strange events, said to have recently taken place in France and other parts of the Continent. Are these accounts of such a character as to allay, or to strengthen and increase, such doubts as have been suggested in the foregoing pages?

We are told that there is now a Napoleon Buonaparte at the head of the government of France. It is not, indeed, asserted that he is the very original Napoleon Buonaparte himself. The death of that personage, and the transportation of his genuine bones to France, had been too widely proclaimed to allow of his reappearance in his own proper person. But "uno avulso, non deficit alter." Like the Thibetian worshippers of the Dalai Lama, (who never dies; only his soul transmigrates into a fresh body), the French are so resolved, we are told, to be under a Buonaparte—whether that be a man or "a system"—that they have found, it seems, a kind of new incarnation of this their Grand Lama, in a person said to be the nephew of the original one.

And when, on hearing that this personage now fills the high office of President of the French Republic, we inquire (very naturally) how he came there, we are informed that, several years ago, he invaded France in an English vessel, (the English—having always been suspected of keeping Buonaparte ready, like the winds in a Lapland witch's bag, to be let out on occasion,) at the head of a force, not, of six hundred men, like his supposed uncle in his expedition from Elba, but of fifty-five,(!) with which he landed at Boulogne, proclaimed himself emperor, and was joined by no less than one man! He was accordingly, we are told, arrested, brought to trial, and sentenced to imprisonment; but having, some years after, escaped from prison, and taken refuge in England, (England again!) he thence returned to France: AND SO the French nation placed him at the head of the government!

All this will doubtless be received as a very probable tale by those who have given full credit to all the stories I have alluded to in the foregoing pages.

Postscript to the Eleventh Edition

When any dramatic piece takes—as the phrase is—with the Public, it will usually be represented again and again with still-continued applause; and sometimes imitations of it will be produced; so that the same drama in substance will, with occasional slight variations in the plot, and changes of names, long keep possession of the stage.

Something like this has taken place with respect to that curious tragi-comedy—the scene of it laid in France—which has engaged the attention of the British public for about sixty years; during which it has been "exhibited to crowded houses"—viz., coffee-houses, reading-rooms, &c., with unabated interest.

The outline of this drama, or series of dramas, may be thus sketched:

DRAMATIS PERSONÆ.

A. *A King or other Sovereign.*
B. *His Queen.*
C. *The Heir apparent.*
D. E. F. *His Ministers.*
G. H. I. J. K. *Demagogues.*
L. *A popular leader of superior ingenuity, who becomes ultimately supreme ruler under the title of Dictator, Consul, Emperor, King, President, or some other. Soldiers, Senators, Executioners, and other functionaries, Citizens, Fishwomen, &c.*

SCENE, PARIS.

(1.) The first Act of one of these dramas represents
a monarchy, somewhat troubled by murmurs of
disaffection, suspicions of conspiracy, &c.
(2.) Second Act, a rebellion; in which ultimately
the government is overthrown.
(3.) Act the third, a provisional government established,
on principles of liberty, equality, fraternity, &c.
(4.) Act the fourth, struggles of various parties for power,
carried on with sundry intrigues, and sanguinary conflicts.
(5.) Act the fifth, the re-establishment of
some form of absolute monarchy.

And from this point we start afresh, and begin the same
business over again, with sundry fresh interludes.

All this is highly amusing to the English Public to hear and
read of; but I doubt whether our countrymen would like to be
actual performers in such a drama.

Whether the French really are so, or whether they are
mystifying us in the accounts they send over, I will not presume
to decide. But if the former supposition be the true one,—if they
have been so long really acting over and over again in their own
persons such a drama, it must be allowed that they deserve to
be characterized as they have been in the description given of
certain European nations: "An Englishman," it has been said,
"is never happy but when he is miserable; a Scotchman is never
at home but when he is abroad; an Irishman is never at peace
but when he is fighting; a Spaniard is never at liberty but when
he is enslaved; and a Frenchman is never settled but when he is
engaged in a revolution."

Postscript to the Twelfth Edition

"Time" says the proverb, "rings Truth to light." But the process is gradual and slow. The debt is paid, as it were, by instalments. It is only bit by bit, and at considerable intervals, that Truth comes forth as the morning twilight to dispel the mists of fiction.

It is above forty years that men have been debating the question:—Who were the parties that burned the city of Moscow?—without ever thinking of the preliminary question, whether it ever was burnt at all. And now at length we learn that it never was.

The following extract from a New Orleans paper contains the information obtained by an American traveller—one of that great nation whose accuracy as to facts is so well known—who visited the spot.

INCIDENTS OF TRAVEL—CITY OF MOSCOW

Senator Douglas is said to have made the discovery, while travelling in Russia, that the city of Moscow was never burned! The following statement of the matter is from the Muscatine (Iowa) Inquirer:

"Coming on the boat, a few days ago, we happened to fall in company with Senator Douglas, who came on board at Quincy, on his way to Warsaw. In the course of a very interesting account of his travels in Russia, much of which has been published by letter-writers, he stated a fact which has never yet been published, but which startlingly contradicts the historical relation of one of the most extraordinary events that ever fell to the lot of history to record. For this reason the Judge said he felt a delicacy in making the assertion, that the city of Moscow was never burned!

"He said, that previous to his arrival at Moscow, he had several disputes with his guide as to the burning of the city, the guide declaring that it never occurred, and seeming to be nettled at Mr. Douglas's persistency in his opinion; but, on examining the fire-marks around the city, and the city itself, he became satisfied that the guide was correct.

"The statement goes on to set forth that the antiquity of the architectural city—particularly of its 'six hundred first-class churches,' stretching through ante-Napoleonic ages to Pagan times, and showing the handiwork of different nations of History—demonstrates that the city never was burned down (or up)."

The Inquirer adds:

"The Kremlin is a space of several hundred acres, in the heart of the city, in the shape of a flat iron, and is enclosed, by a wall of sixty feet high. Within this enclosure is the most magnificent palace in Europe, recently built, but constructed over an ancient palace, which remains, thus enclosed, whole and perfect, with all its windows, &c.

"Near the Kremlin, surrounded by a wall, is a Chinese town, appearing to be several hundred years old, still occupied by descendants of the original settlers.

"The circumstances which gave rise to the errors concerning the burning of Moscow, were these:—It is a city of four hundred and fifty thousand inhabitants, in circular form, occupying a large space, five miles across. There the winters are six months long, and the custom was, and still is, to lay up supplies of provisions and wood to last six months of severe cold weather. To prevent these gigantic supplies from encumbering the heart of the city, and yet render them as convenient as practicable to every locality, a row of wood houses was constructed to circle completely round the city, and outside of these was a row of granaries, and in these were deposited the whole of the supplies. Napoleon had entered the city with his army, and was himself occupying the palace of the Kremlin, when, one night, by order of the Russian governor, every wood house and every granary simultaneously burst into a blaze. All efforts to extinguish them were vain, and Napoleon found himself compelled to march his army through the fire. Retiring to an eminence he saw the whole city enveloped in vast sheets of flame, and clouds of smoke, and apparently all on fire. And far as he was concerned it might as well have been, for though houses enough were left to supply every soldier with a room, yet without provisions or fuel, and a Russian army to cut off supplies, he and his army could not subsist there. During the fire some houses were probably burnt, but the city was not. In the Kremlin a magazine blew up, cracking the church of Ivan more than a hundred feet up, but setting nothing on fire.

"Mr. Douglas saw the fire-marks around the city, where wood houses and granaries for winter supplies now stand as of old; but there appears no marks of conflagration within the city."

Any wary sceptic, indeed, might have found much ground for doubt in the very accounts themselves that were given of the conflagration. For, the Russians have always denied that they burned it; and the French equally disclaimed the act. Each of the two parties between whom the accusation lay, strenuously denied it. And it must be acknowledged that each had very strong presumptions of innocence to urge. It was certainly most unlikely that the Russians should themselves destroy their ancient and venerable capital; and that, too, when they were boasting of having just gained a great victory at Borodino over an army which, therefore, they might hope to defeat again, and to drive out of their city. And it was no less unlikely that the French should burn down a city of which they had possession, and which afforded shelter and refreshment to their troops. This would have been one of the most improbable circumstances of that most improbable (supposed) campaign. To add to the marvel, we are told that the French army nevertheless waited for five weeks, without any object, amid the ashes of this destroyed city, just at the approach, of winter, and as if on purpose to be overtaken and destroyed by snows and frost!

However, all the difficulties of the question whether any of these things took place at all, were by most persons overlooked, because the question itself never occurred to them, in their eagerness to decide who it was that burned the city. And at length it comes out that the answer is, Nobody!

FOOTNOTES IN THE ORIGINAL:

[1] "A report is spread, (says Voltaire in one of his works,) that there is, in some country or other, a giant as big as a mountain; and men presently fall to hot disputing concerning the precise length of his nose, the breadth of his thumb, and other particulars, and anathematize each other for heterodoxy of belief concerning them. In the midst of all, if some bold sceptic ventures to hint a doubt as to the existence of this giant, all are ready to join against him, and tear him to pieces." This looks almost like a prophetic allegory relating to the gigantic Napoleon.

[2] Οὕτως ἀταλαίπωρος τοῖς πολλοῖς ἡ ζήτησις τῆς ἀληθείας, καὶ ἐπὶ τὰ ἕτοιμα μᾶλλον τρέπονται. Thucyd. b.i.c. 20.

[3] "With what greediness are the miraculous accounts of travellers received, their descriptions of sea and land monsters, their relations of wonderful adventures, strange men, and uncouth manners!"—Hume's Essay on Miracles, p. 179, 12mo; p. 185, 8vo, 1767; p. 117, 8vo, 1817. N.B.—In order to give every possible facility of reference, three editions of Hume's Essays have been generally employed: a 12mo, London, 1756, and two 8vo editions.

[4] "Suppose a fact to be transmitted through twenty persons; the first communicating it to the second, the second to the third, &c., and let the probability of each testimony be expressed by nine-tenths, (that is, suppose that of ten reports made by each witness, nine only are true,) then, at every time the story passes from one witness to another, the evidence is reduced to nine-tenths of what it was before. Thus, after it has passed through the whole twenty, the evidence will be found to be less than one-eighth."—La Place, Essai Philosophique sur les Probabilités. That is, the chances for the fact thus attested being true, will be, according to this distinguished calculator, less than one in eight. Very few of the common newspaper-stories, however, relating to

218

foreign countries, could be traced, if the matter were carefully investigated, up to an actual eye-witness, even through twenty intermediate witnesses; and many of the steps of our ladder, would, I fear, prove but rotten; few of the reporters would deserve to have one in ten fixed as the proportion of their false accounts.

[5] "I did not mention the difficulty of detecting a falsehood in any private or even public history, at the time and place where it is said to happen; much more where the scene is removed to ever so small a distance . . . But the matter never comes to any issue, if trusted to the common method of altercation and debate and flying rumours."—Hume's Essay on Miracles, p. 195, 12mo; pp. 200, 201, 8vo, 1767; p. 127, 8vo, 1817.

[6] See the third Postscript appended to this edition.

[7] "We entertain a suspicion concerning any matter of fact, when the witnesses contradict each other; when they are of a suspicious character; when they have an interest in what they affirm."— Hume's Essay on Miracles, p. 172, 12mo; p. 176, 8vo, 1767; p. 113, 8vo. 1817.

[8] "That testimony itself derives all its force from experience, seems very certain . . . The first author, we believe, who stated fairly the connexion between the evidence of testimony and the evidence of experience, was Hume, in his Essay on Miracles, a work ... abounding in maxims of great use in the conduct of life."—Edin. Review, Sept. 1814, p. 328.

[9] "Suppose, for instance, that the fact which the testimony endeavours to establish partakes of the extraordinary and the marvellous; in that case, the evidence resulting from the testimony receives a diminution, greater or less in proportion as the fact is more or less unusual."—Hume's Essay on Miracles, p. 173, 12mo; p. 176, 8vo, 1767; p. 113, 8vo, 1817.

[10] "The ultimate standard by which we determine all disputes that may arise is always derived from experience and observation."—Hume's Essay on Miracles, p. 172, 12mo; p. 175, 8vo, 1767; p. 112, 8vo, 1817.

[11] Ἡ θαύματα πολλά. Καὶ τού τι καὶ βροτῶν φρένας ὙΠΕΡ ΤΟΝ ΑΛΗΘΗ ΛΟΓΟΝ Δεδειδαλμένοι ψεύδεσι ποικίλοις Ἐξαπατῶντι μῦθοι.—Pind. Olymp.

[12] This doctrine, though hardly needing confirmation from authority, is supported by that of Hume; his eighth essay is, throughout, an argument for the doctrine of "Philosophical necessity," drawn entirely from the general uniformity, observable in the course of nature with respect to the principles of human conduct, as well as those of the material universe; from which uniformity, he observes, it is that we are enabled in both cases, to form our judgment by means of Experience: "and if," says he, "we would explode any forgery in history, we cannot make use of a more convincing argument, than to prove that the actions ascribed to any person, are directly contrary to the course of nature . . . " The Veracity of Quintus Curtius is as suspicious when he describes the supernatural courage of Alexander, by which he was hurried on singly to attack multitudes, as when he describes his supernatural force and activity, by which he was able to resist them. So readily and universally do we acknowledge a uniformity in human motives and actions, as well as in the operations of body."—Eighth Essay, p. 131, 12mo; p. 85, 8vo, 1817. Accordingly, in the tenth essay, his use of the term "miracle," after having called it "a transgression of a law of nature," plainly shows that he meant to include human nature: "no testimony," says he, "is sufficient to establish a miracle, unless the testimony be of such a nature that its falsehood would be more miraculous than the fact which it endeavours to establish." The term "prodigy" also (which he all along employs as synonymous with "miracle") is applied to testimony, in the same manner, immediately after; "In

the foregoing reasoning we have supposed ... that the falsehood of that testimony would be a kind of prodigy." Now had he meant to confine the meaning of "miracle," and "prodigy," to a violation of the laws of matter, the epithet "miraculous," applied even thus hypothetically, to false testimony, would be as unmeaning as the epithets "green" or "square;" the only possible sense in which we can apply to it, even in imagination, the term "miraculous," is that of "highly improbable,"—"contrary to those laws of nature which respect human conduct:" and in this sense he accordingly uses the word in the very next sentence: "When any one tells me that he saw a dead man restored to life, I immediately consider with myself whether it be more probable that this person should either deceive or be deceived, or that the fact which he relates should really have happened. I weigh the one miracle against the other."—Hume's Essay on Miracles, pp. 176, 177, 12mo; p. 182, 8vo, 1767; p. 115, 8vo, 1817. See also a passage above quoted from the same essay, where he speaks of "the miraculous accounts of travellers;" evidently using the word in this sense. Perhaps it was superfluous to cite authority for applying the term "miracle" to whatever is "highly improbable;" but it is important to the students of Hume, to be fully aware that he uses those two expressions as synonymous; since otherwise they would mistake the meaning of that passage which he justly calls "a general maxim worthy of your attention."

[13] "Events may be so extraordinary that they can hardly be established by testimony. We would not give credit to a man who would affirm that he saw a hundred dice thrown in the air, and that they all fell on the same faces."—Edin. Review, Sept. 1814, p. 327.

[14] If the spirit of religion join itself to the love of wonder, there is an end of common sense; and human testimony in these circumstances loses all pretensions to authority."—Hume's Essay on Miracles, p. 179, 12mo; p. 185, 8vo, 1767; p. 117, 8vo, 1817.

[15] The supposed history from which the above extracts are given, is published entire in the work called Historic Certainties.

[16] "I desire any one to lay his hand upon his heart, and after serious consideration declare whether he thinks that the falsehood of such a book, supported by such testimony, would be more extraordinary and miraculous than all the miracles it relates."— Hume's Essay on Miracles, p. 200, 12mo; p. 206, 8vo, 1767; p. 131, 8vo, 1817. Let it be observed, that the instance here given is miraculous in no other sense but that of being highly improbable.

[17] "The wise lend a very academic faith to every report which favours the passion of the reporter, whether it magnifies his country, his family, or himself."—Hume's Essay on Miracles, p. 144, 12mo; p. 200, 8vo, 1767; p. 126, 8vo, 1817.

[18] "Nothing can be more contrary than such a philosophy (the academic or sceptical) to the supine indolence of the mind, its rash arrogance, its lofty pretensions, and its superstitious credulity."—Fifth Essay, p. 68, 12mo; p. 41, 8vo, 1817.

[19] See Hume's Essay on Miracles, pp. 189, 191, 195, 12mo; pp. 193, 197, 201, 202, 8vo, 1767; pp. 124, 125, 126, 8vo, 1817.

[20] See Edinburgh Review for October, 1842, p. 162.

[21] See Edinburgh Review for October, 1842, p. 162.

[22] Germaniæ vocabulum recens et nuper additum; quoniam qui primi Rhenum transgressi Gallos expulerint, ac nunc Tungri, tunc Germani vocati sint: ita nationis nomen in nomen gentis evaluisse paullatim, ut omnes, primum a victore ob metum, mox a seipsis invento nomine, Germani vocarentur.—Tacitus, de Mor. Germ.

Printed in Great Britain
by Amazon